London Moxie

Be an insider.

First Edition 2005

Bethany Carlson

Metropolis Moxie

www.metropolismoxie.com

Metropolis Moxie
PO Box 19477
Seattle WA 98109
206.285.0056
www.metropolismoxie.com

© 2005 by Bethany Carlson

ISBN 0-9770334-0-6
LCN 2005930178

All rights reserved. No part of this publication may be reproduced or used in any form or by any means, graphic, electronic, or mechanical, including photocopying, recording, taping, or information storage without written permission of the publisher.

Metropolis Moxie, Be an insider., and the Metropolis Moxie logo are trademarks of Metropolis Moxie pending registration in the US Patent and Trademark Office.

This publication is designed to provide accurate and authoritative information in regard to the subject matter covered. However, the authors and publisher make no warranty about the accuracy or completeness of its content and, to the maximum extent permitted, disclaim all liability arising from its use.

Metropolis Moxie books provide independent advice. Metropolis Moxie does not accept advertising in guidebooks, nor do we accept payment in exchange for listing or endorsing any place or business. Metropolis Moxie writers do not accept discounts or payments in exchange for positive coverage of any sort.

Please direct any comments, questions, or suggestions regarding this book to: metropolismoxie@metropolismoxie.com.

Author: Bethany Carlson
Editor: Roberta Cruger
Cover Designer: Brad Weikel
Logo Designers: Robyn Winters and Jennifer Aldrich

Printed in the United States of America

it's time London became your home away from home

Be an Insider

These days, being called a tourist is almost an insult.

The problem is that most travel 'guides' are more like *directories*. They're full of addresses and recommendations, but they don't turn a new city into your next home away from home. This makes it only too easy to take the amusement park approach to a city like London and get stuck in the tourist rut.

But although it may at first appear daunting, an unfamiliar city really can become easily manageable with the right deciphering. All you need is a good translation of its layout – where are the arts quarters, the financial center, the shopping districts, the residential areas? Once you know which neighborhoods interest you (and which to avoid), are armed with a good map and prepped on the transportation system, you can approach London with confidence. Throw in a few extras like when and what people eat and drink, what to wear and who's popular on TV, and you can call the city your own.

Stepping off the tourist merry-go-round has so many benefits: more relaxation, shorter lines, fewer scams, more reality, and – most importantly – the opportunity to make acquaintances and, if you're lucky, friends. Since you can't ever hope to see everything in London, pick a few priorities, see them in the morning when you're fresh and queues are shorter, and then take the afternoon to just hang out and soak it in, leaving the door open for an encounter to turn into a conversation, a conversation into an invitation, and a night out at the pub into a memory you'll savor years after you return home.

So, why be a tourist? Whether you'll be there for a day or a year, Metropolis Moxie wants you to experience London as an insider. We are more than happy to show you how.

Pure London Moxie

mox·ie (mŏk'sē)
n. Slang
1. The ability to face difficulty with spirit and courage.
2. Aggressive energy; initiative.
3. Skill; know-how.

Me·trop·o·lis Mox·ie (mĭ-trŏp'ə-lĭs mŏk'sē)
n. Proper Noun
1. Insider knowledge to approach a new city with confidence.

Lon·don Mox·ie (lŭn'dən mŏk'sē)
n. Proper Noun

1. **Dress Well** London is a fashion capital of the world. If ever there was a time to absolutely indulge in clothes, this is it! They make great souvenirs, so bring money to shop.

2. **Get Savvy** Londoners aren't unfriendly; they just place high value on wit and being current on world affairs (things Americans are not typically known for). Check up on the latest news and gossip before going so you can engage in smart conversation.

3. **Pursue Your Passion** London has a little of everything, often at its pinnacle. It's worth the time to do the homework to find a club, store, museum, or group dedicated to what you love.

4. **Pick a Neighborhood** London is an intricate knot of neighborhoods, each with its own flavor. Don't waste time commuting and missing out on the local fun – stick to one area per day and walk, walk, walk.

5. **Get a Proper Map** Getting lost in London is inevitable without a proper map. The spiral-bound *London mini A-Z* is what Londoners use, so borrow one or buy it at www.a-zmaps.co.uk.

A Note from Ms. Moxie

Hi! I'm so excited you're coming to London.

I love to travel. After seven years of working around the world as an investment analyst (including a two-year stint in London), I finally turned out the fluorescent lights at my cubicle for the last time and dedicated myself to a cause: making sure no traveler had to ever again unwittingly bear the stigma of the American tourist reputation.

The seed was planted in Madrid during the summer of 1992. On this, my first solo trip overseas at the tender age of 15, I was confronted with several facts: 1. Americans are clearly recognizable from a mile away when we wear super-casual attire and speak in loud voices; 2. Being instantly recognized as such is a liability abroad, as we can be unpopular because of our power (and politics); 3. It was easy to get people to assume I was a Madrileña by behaving like one; and 4. I had way more fun in Madrid as a Madrileña rather than an American!

Since that summer I've had the opportunity to hone the skill of going from outsider to insider time and again. It's a little difficult for Americans to perform this chameleon act, thanks to our cultural focus on independence rather than blending in. But I strongly encourage any traveler to keep trying. With Metropolis Moxie and a little practice, you too can find yourself on the inside and come to love London as a second home.

Very happy travels and stay fabulous always,

-Bethany

A Day in the Life of a Londoner

- **6am** Rise and watch Breakfast on BBC One whilst enjoying a bowl of Wheatabix.
- **7** Mad dash, long queues, and cramped quarters on the Tube, trains and buses – most days start in someone else's armpit.
- **8** At the office suits are *de rigueur*. Men do not fear pastel shirts and ties.
- **9** Ring business associates in Sydney, Tokyo and Hong Kong.
- **10** No cubicles here, so chat over the desk with workmates about last night's episodes of Hollyoaks and Big Brother.
- **11** Nip out to the shop for a snack to cure the elevenses.
- **12pm** Get some actual work accomplished.
- **1** Head down to the pub or the caff for a jacket potato lunch.
- **2** Ring business associates in New York and Boston.
- **3** Tune in (very quietly!) online to the Arsenal : Manchester United match.
- **4** Time for a little more genuine exertion.
- **5** Pick up an *Evening Standard* for up-to-date headlines on the ride home. The workday ends, as it began, in someone else's armpit.
- **6** Go to the gym and clock off a few miles on the treadmill.
- **7** Restock the fridge with purchases from the Sainsbury's or Tesco, and the medicine cabinet with supplies from Boots.
- **8** Down to the local pub for some bangers 'n' mash and a chat with the regulars.
- **9** Have a few pints and lose a few quid on the Golden Tee and fruit machines. Next time lucky!
- **10** Impress the fit bird (or bloke) who walked in with white-hot wit.
- **11** Pub closes. Nightie night!

Using this Guide

Coordinates show the relevant pages in the spiral bound *London mini A-Z*, Tube stations, and bus routes to adjacent neighborhoods.

COORDINATES

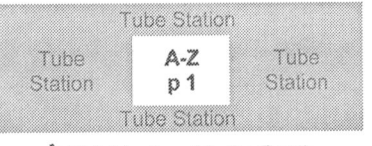

Profiles summarize the best attributes of the neighborhood.

PROFILE

Special Dates	Day				Night			
Listed here are events that only happen once a year.	See	Shop	Stroll	Relax	Watch	Eat	Party	Unwind
		✓		✓		✓		

Dossiers provide background and tips on approaching a visit to each neighborhood.

DOSSIER

Go:	Is this a good weekend or weekday, day or night place?
Recognize:	What London icons can be seen here?
Expect:	Is this place loud, busy, quaint, modern, or what?
Wear:	How do Londoners dress in this neighborhood?
Avoid:	Are there any dangerous or unpleasant areas around?
Know:	What are the unique characteristics of this place?

Using the Guide

Each neighborhood is full of recommendations on what to see and do throughout the day. But there's no fluff or filler – if there isn't anything to do in a particular area on a weekday or Saturday night, we say so!

In the morning:
The morning is the best time to sightsee, when you are well-rested and before the hordes descend. Museums, monuments, icons, and busy shopping areas are included in the morning section.

For lunch:
Particularly in areas frequented by tourists, there is an abundance of bad and expensive food. We provide recommendations on quick eats, fancy meals, picnics – whatever's appropriate to the area.

In the afternoon:
There's only so much 'culture' one can absorb in a day. In the afternoon we suggest places to stroll, sit, people watch, pub crawl, take tea, shop, and basically let the world roll by.

For dinner:
We provide specific recommendations for stand-out favorites and point out areas where you're spoiled for choice. Restaurant prices are given as per person for starter, main course, and a glass of wine.

In the evening:
London is teeming with activity when the sun goes down. Here we list entertainment, sports, pubs, clubs, bars, 'n more for your enjoyment.

Index
At the end of each neighborhood is an index with all contact, website, price, and opening time information.

Table of Contents

The Neighborhoods

14 Hampstead/Camden p70

15 Islington p74

11 Bloomsbury/Clerkenwell p58

10 Marylebone/Fitzrovia p52

12 Shoreditch/Spitalfields p62

Bayswater

9 Holland Park/Notting Hill p48

3 Covent Garden/Strand p23

2 Mayfair/Soho p18

4 Holborn/Embankment p26

5 City p30

RIVER THAMES

8 Knightsbridge/S. Kensington p44

1 Westminster p14

6 Southwark/Lambeth p34

→ **16** Greenwich p79

7 Chelsea/Fulham p40

13 Brixton/Clapham p66

Farther Afield – Day Trips and Getaways	83

The Resources

Plan Your Trip	88
Book This Now	91
*Accommodation (Bayswater)	92
Specialty Guides	96
Get Oriented	97
Get Around	98
Get Connected	100
Make Friends	102
Down the Pub	107
Speak Well	110
Save Money	113
Discover Secret London	117
Emergency Information / Personal Safety	119

The Index

120

Table of Contents

Neighborhood	See	Shop	Stroll	Relax	Watch	Eat	Party	Unwind
1 Westminster	✓		✓		✓			
2 Mayfair/Soho		✓			✓	✓	✓	
3 Covent Garden/Strand					✓			
4 Holborn/Embankment	✓		✓					
5 City	✓		✓					
6 Southwark/Lambeth	✓		✓	✓	✓		✓	✓
7 Chelsea/Fulham		✓	✓	✓	✓	✓		✓
8 Knightsbridge/South Ken	✓	✓	✓	✓	✓	✓	✓	
9 Holland Park/Notting Hill		✓	✓	✓				
10 Marylebone/Fitzrovia	✓	✓	✓	✓	✓	✓	✓	✓
11 Bloomsbury/Clerkenwell	✓			✓		✓	✓	✓
12 Shoreditch/Spitalfields	✓	✓				✓	✓	
13 Brixton/Clapham			✓	✓		✓	✓	✓
14 Hampstead/Camden		✓	✓	✓	✓	✓		
15 Islington		✓	✓	✓	✓	✓	✓	✓
16 Greenwich	✓		✓	✓				✓

Neighborhoods are listed by location in a clockwise spiral, starting from Big Ben in the center, then moving north and east. Central areas are heavy on icons – and tourists; those farther out are more residential and laid-back. Each is evaluated on eight categories:

- **See**: Major icons, museums, and sights
- **Shop**: Clothes, souvenir, and/or specialty shopping
- **Stroll**: Scenic walks and/or open green space
- **Relax**: Leisurely places to sit and watch the world go by
- **Watch**: Major entertainment or sports
- **Eat**: Specific favorite restaurants or good restaurant browsing
- **Party**: Hip bars and clubs open late
- **Unwind**: Low-key pubs and hang-outs

Great Itineraries

There's never enough time to see everything in London, so here are suggestions on narrowing the field.

Modern Art Cognoscenti Southwark-6 +Marylebone-10 +Shoreditch-12
Tate Modern, Saatchi, White Cube, and A+D showcase today's geniuses.

Classical Art Aficionados Westminster-1 +Marylebone-10 +Embankment-11
National Gallery, Wallace Collection, and Somerset House delight the eye.

Architects, Votaries and Bureaucrats Westminster-1 +Holborn-4 +City-5
One thousand years of masterpieces legal, political, and ecclesiastical.

History Buffs Westminster-1 +City-5 +Bloomsbury-11
Relive the past through the treasures of Westminster, the Tower, Museum of London, British Museum and the British Library.

Antique Hunters Notting Hill-9 +Camden-14 +Islington-15
The search is on at Portobello, Camden Markets, and Camden Passage.

Fashionistas Mayfair-2 +Chelsea-7 +Knightsbridge-8
The stylish flock to Oxford and Bond Streets, King's and Fulham Roads, Sloane Square, and all shop fronts in between.

Boutique Browsers Notting Hill-9 +Shoreditch-12 +Islington-15
Foreswear the labels on Ledbury, Cheshire, Cross, and Upper Streets.

Market Explorers Southwark-6 +Spitalfields-12 +Camden-14
Fine food, clothes, and wares await at Borough, Spitalfields, Camden Town.

Perambulators Southwark-6 +Marylebone-10 +Hampstead-14
Enjoy river views, charming buildings, leafy streets, and roomy pathways in these lovely neighborhoods.

Green Thumbs Lambeth-6 +Chelsea-7 +Holland Park-9
Delight in the Museum of Garden History, the magical Chelsea Physic Garden, and the pleasant pathways of Holland Park.

Great Itineraries

Vista Viewers Southwark-6 +Marylebone-10 +Hampstead-14
Admire the skyline from high hills, the Thames' bridges and the London Eye.

Tea Takers Mayfair-2 +Southwark-6 +Kensington-8
Silver, china, crumpets, cakes, and cucumber sandwiches. Lovely!

Contemporary Music Groupies Brixton-13 +Camden-14
Brixton Academy sells out early, check out new names in Camden Town.

Classical Music Devotees Covent Garden-3 +Southwark-6 +Marylebone-10
Royal Opera House, Royal Festival Hall, and Wigmore Hall please the ear.

Contemporary Theater Enthusiasts Soho-2 +Islington-15
Big names in Soho, first runs in Islington – London's full of new drama.

Classical Theater Disciples Soho-2 +Covent Garden-3 +Southwark-6
London is theater's home – don't miss the perfectly accurate Globe.

Sport Fans Fulham 7 +Marylebone-10 +Islington-15
Cheer on *real* football and cricket at Chelsea, Arsenal, and Lord's.

Bar Hoppers Soho-2 +Fitzrovia-10 +Clerkenwell-11
Don fashionable threads and enjoy martinis in the hippest watering holes.

Clubbers Clerkenwell-11 +Shoreditch-12 +Brixton-13
There's no lack of company for black lights and untz-untz 'til 5am.

Pint Lovers Southwark-6 +Clerkenwell-11 +Islington-15
Pubs abound in London, but these neighborhoods are made for crawls.

Bethany's London Westminster-1 +Mayfair-2 +Islington-15
Relive Bethany's years with a stroll down Tothill Street to St. James's Park, shop Oxford Street till you drop, then have a pint at The Canonbury.

Don't know where to start? London Walks Company tours provide fun, fast, and fact-filled intros to London's neighborhoods.   www.walks.com

1 Westminster

COORDINATES

↑ *2 Mayfair / Soho*
Buses: 3, 12, 24, 88, 159, 453

↑**N**

← *8 Knightsbridge / South Kensington* *11, 211*

Tube Stations: Charing Cross

| St. James's Park | **A-Z** **p 75-76** | Westminster |

Pimlico

→ *6 Southwark / Lambeth* *12, 53, 211, 148, 453*

↓ *N/A*

PROFILE

Special Dates	Day				Night			
Autumn: State opening of Parliament. See the Queen in the golden coach. www.parliament.uk	See	Shop	Stroll	Relax	Watch	Eat	Party	Unwind
	✓		✓		✓			

DOSSIER

Go:	Weekday sightseeing; visiting all sites will take two days.
Recognize:	Big Ben, Westminster Abbey, Buckingham Palace, Nelson's Column and the lions
Expect:	Queues, noise, awe, history, government, royals, religion
Wear:	Smart, simple, comfortable for standing and walking; alternatively, wear a suit to blend in with the working folks.
Avoid:	Lingering at Victoria station
Know:	Westminster is the most icon-laden locale in London. Big Ben and crew really deliver, and a day in Westminster will make you say to yourself "I'm in London! I'm really in London!" Hence all the tourists. Missing Westminster would be a huge mistake, but don't dwell here either.

Westminster 1

In the morning:
The **National Gallery** is a prince of classical art museums, with exceptional collections and curators. Arriving just before 10 am should ensure enough time to enjoy your favorite art movement before the crowds descend. Art devotees will want to stop at the adjoining **National Portrait Gallery**, which houses both historic and contemporary portraits of Britain's notables.

An alternative for those who have already visited the NG is the **Tate Britain**, an excellent and extensive museum devoted to British artists. The Tate is south of Parliament Square and most easily accessed from Pimlico Tube.

For lunch:
The National Gallery boasts a commendable cafe and restaurant, the Tate Britain even more so. A cheap and cheerful alternative is the **Crypt Café** at St. Martin-in-the-Fields, also on Trafalgar Square. Those heading to Parliament Square should consider one of the many pubs and cafes around St. James's Park Tube station, or getting a "take away" (to go) lunch at dependable chains **EAT** or **Pret a Manger** to eat *al fresco* in lovely **St. James's Park**, the Queen's beautifully manicured public front garden[1].

In the afternoon:
Music aficionados will want to take advantage of the free lunchtime concerts held at **St. Martin-in-the-Fields** and the bandstand at St. James's Park. Performance frequency and times vary seasonally, so check the websites in advance. The park is a lovely place even on non-concert days for a relaxing stroll.

---

[1] St. James's Park offers a particularly attractive view of Buckingham Palace. Visiting the palace itself requires good timing, enduring long queues, and battling hordes of tourists on top of the £13.50 entry fee. A less-crowded and more interesting alternative is the Royal Mews, which houses all of the royal vehicles, including the state golden coach. www.royalcollection.org.uk → Visit → Royal Mews

Anyone finding a Londoner at the changing of the guard should win a prize.

1 Westminster

History buffs and those wanting to learn more about WWII will certainly want to visit the informative and goose-bump raising **Cabinet War Rooms** and newly opened **Churchill Museum**, both housed in the same basement building in Whitehall at the west end of St. James's Park.

Westminster Abbey, one of the ecclesiastical icons of the world, still lives on as a house of worship. Sightseers should arrive at the Abbey around 1:30 to ensure a spot in either the 2 pm or 2:30 tour, which lasts 90 minutes and includes all adjacent church buildings and points of interest. The church closes to tourists at 4:45 in preparation for the 5 pm evensong. Worshipers should arrive by 4:30 to claim a seat for this brief but incredibly beautiful service. Special events can interrupt the usual schedule at any time of the year, so check the website in advance.

For dinner:
Consider one of the legions of pubs in the region bordered north and south by Victoria Street and St. James's Park, east and west by Victoria station and St. James's Park tube. Stick to classic pub fare (e.g., bangers & mash) and avoid pastas and curries.

In the evening:
Big Ben at the **Palace of Westminster** is *the* symbol of London. After major refurbishments at the millennium, both look their best in decades. Even better are the debates taking place inside. All are welcome to visit the Public (or "Strangers'") Galleries of both the House of Lords and the House of Commons. The schedule is somewhat erratic, so it is necessary to check the website in advance, but a great time to go is Monday evening between October and July when the arguments rage until 8:30 pm or later. During the summer recess tours of the building are available all day.

Westminster 1

Index:
- All times are daily unless noted otherwise, and are subject to change.
- Obtaining a reservation or place on the guest list is always recommended.

The National Gallery, Trafalgar Square, WC2N 5DN
+44 (0)20 7747 2885
www.nationalgallery.org.uk / £Free
10am-6pm; to 9pm on W / café, restaurant (lunch, early dinner)

National Portrait Gallery, St Martin's Place, WC2H OHE
+44 (0)20 7306 0055
www.npg.org.uk / £Free
10- 6; to 9 on Th-F / café, view restaurant (lun daily; din Th-F only)

Crypt Café & St Martin-in-the-Fields, Trafalgar Square, WC2N 4JJ
+44 (0)20 7766 1129
www.stmartin-in-the-fields.org
£6 / Café open 10am-8pm; to 11pm Th-St; open at noon on Sn

EAT www.eatcafe.co.uk

Pret a Manger www.pret.com

Tate Britain, Millbank, SW1P 4RG
+44 (0)20 7887 8000
www.tate.org.uk / £Free
10am-5:50pm / café, view restaurant (breakfast, lunch, tea)

St. James's Park, SW1
www.royalparks.gov.uk
5pm-midnight / café

Cabinet War Rooms & Churchill Museum, Clive Steps, King Charles Street, SW1A 2AQ
+44 (0)20 7930 6961
www.iwm.org.uk / £10 / 9:30am-6pm
café

Westminster Abbey, 20, Deans Yard, SW1P 3PA
+44 (0)20 7222 5152
www.westminster-abbey.org
£8 / times vary, check website
Usually: Open 9:30am-3:45pm M-St; to 7pm W. Tours 10, 11, 2, 2:30 M-F; 10, 10:30, 11 St. Evensong 5pm M-St, 3pm Sn. Various services Sn

Big Ben & the Palace of Westminster (Parliament)
House of Commons, SW1A 0AA
House of Lords, SW1A 0PW
+44 (0)20 7219 3000
www.parliament.uk
Strangers' Gallery £Free, summer tours £7 / times vary, check the website in advance

2 Mayfair / Soho

COORDINATES

↑ *10 Marylebone / Fitzrovia*
Buses: 13, 113, 139, 189

↑**N**

← *Hyde Park* 8, 9, 10, 14, 19, 38, 73, 137	Tube Stations: Bond Street, Oxford Circus Tottenham Court Road Green Park — **A-Z p 74-75** — Leicester Square Piccadilly Circus

→ *11 Bloomsbury / Clerkenwell*
7, 8, 25, 19, 38, 55, 98

↓ *1 Westminster*
3, 12, 88, 159, 453

PROFILE

Special Dates	Day				Night			
	See	Shop	Stroll	Relax	Watch	Eat	Party	Unwind
Jan/Jul: Clothing shop sales Feb: Chinese New Year www.chinatownchinese.com		✓			✓	✓	✓	

DOSSIER

Go:	Weekday shopping. Nightly partying, especially weekends
Recognize:	Labels from the top-end on down
Expect:	Crowds, noise, tacky souvenirs, great shopping and bars
Wear:	Trendy to shop and to party. Shoes challenging, requiring balance between comfort for walking and style for impact.
Avoid:	Eastern Oxford Street, Piccadilly Circus, Peter Street
Know:	Mayfair and Soho, divided by Regent Street, are day and night. Mayfair is *posh* - home to original McQueen and Westwood boutiques; Soho is London's answer to New Orleans' Bourbon Street. The northern border of both is Oxford Street – high street shopping par excellence. It's all good fun, BUT: watch your pockets, bad food is a constant threat, and don't expect any R&R.

Mayfair / Soho 2

In the morning:
Only one purpose here: to shop. Oxford Street quickly becomes a zoo, so arrive at Oxford Circus at 9 am to hit **Top Shop**, the affordable trend resource. Westward to Selfridges find every high street chain in London. Keep an eye open for **Next**, purveyor of stylish business attire, **Oasis**, like Top Shop grown up, **FCUK**, for a cheeky Tee, and **Accessorize**, for a bag to go with every new outfit. This is about as affordable as high street shopping gets – figure £50 shoes, £40 jeans, £35 tops, £150 suits.

Note: Most shops do not open until noon on Sundays.

For lunch:
Just north of Oxford Circus find several of the dependable chains: **Caffe Nero**, **Eat**, and **Coffee Republic**, which save hassle and expense. For a high-end option, consider the **Heights** at the St. Georges Hotel, one of only a handful of dining options with a truly panoramic London view.

In the afternoon:
Shopping continues. While the crowds boil on Oxford Street, escape south down Bond Street (both New and Old), somewhat less manic thanks to the price tags. Designer bargain hunters should not miss **Browns Labels for Less**. Fashionistas would regret skipping the opportunity to schmooze with models at UK's own **Vivienne Westwood** and **Alexander McQueen**. Label whores will be in high heaven for blocks. This is as expensive as London shopping gets, figure £500 shoes, £400 jeans, £350 tops, and for one-of-a-kind items the sky's the limit. Circle back to reality along Regent Street for a worthwhile visit to **Liberty**, as much for its delicious Tudor building as its sumptuous clothes. Brit-com addicts can get their fix at the **BBC Shop** – just remember that US VCRs take different tapes, so unless you have a multi-regional player, DVDs won't translate. Serious fashionistas should make an appointment at **Jimmy Choo's** couture studio for a pair of personally designed Choos.

2 Mayfair / Soho

A perfect finale to a hard day's shop is afternoon tea at **Fortnum & Mason** – "grocer" to the Queen by royal warrant since 1707 for good reason. No detail is overlooked from the silver to the china to the cucumber sandwiches to their signature teas.

For dinner:
Fantastic French food in a hiply unhip and warm atmosphere is to be had at the **Pierre Victoire**, just south of Oxford Street. A safe chain for dinner is **Pizza Express**, the one in Soho having the added bonus of an excellent jazz club downstairs. For a hyper-chic alternative, make reservations at **The Ivy** immediately – it's the most likely place in London to spy a celebrity. Soho is one area where relying on a trusted reference is a must, since terrible food abounds.

In the evening:
At the southern end of Soho lies **Theatreland**, home to many of the best playhouses in the world and beloved by great actors everywhere[1]. If you plan to see a show, it's worth checking the **Official London Theatre** website before your trip to see what's on, and go the day-of to the half-price ticket booth, **tkts**, in Leicester Square at 9:45 am. Beware imitators, watch your pockets, and don't linger. If you have your heart set on a particular show or date, purchase tickets ahead of time for peace of mind, since many performances run for a limited time and sell out, sometimes months in advance.

Soho may be best known for its nightlife, which ranges from trampy to swanky and makes for a great bar crawl – style required, leave your jeans back at the B&B. It's advisable to hit the websites of the clubs ahead of time to get on guest lists and skip the queues.

---

[1] It's also home to a few anomalies, such as Agatha Christie's *Mousetrap*. At over a half-century it's the longest-running play in the world, the real mystery here is why. Only some things get better with age.

Mayfair / Soho 2

For a glittery glam night, newcomer **W'Sens** is a smashing place for a cocktail to start off the evening, with perfectly crafted atmosphere and knowledgeable bar staff. Kick things up a notch at **Tiger Tiger** for several floors of bars with beautiful people you can attempt to impress with your chat while sipping a naughtily-named drink. When you're ready to get your groove on, brave Piccadilly Circus to hit **On Anon** for several stories of dance floors open till 3 am.

If these places are too crowded, head north to Heddon Street and Hanover Square, both just west of Regent Street, for dance clubs, including pop favorites **Loop Bar**, **Fiesta Havana**, and **Paragon**. For a break from the furor, head south to Chinatown for **Waxy O'Conners**, an immense Irish pub with a tree growing straight up the middle of it.

Top Shop www.topshop.co.uk

Next www.next.co.uk

Oasis www.oasis-stores.com

FCUK (French Connection)
www.frenchconnection.com

Accessorize
www.accessorize.co.uk

Caffe Nero www.caffenero.co.uk

EAT www.eatcafe.co.uk

Coffee Republic
www.coffeerepublic.co.uk

Heights at the St. Georges Hotel,
Langham Place, W1B 2QS
+44 (0)20 7580 0111
www.saintgeorgeshotel.com
£15 breakfast, £10 lunch, £30 dinner
7am-9.30pm

Browns Labels for Less, 50 South
Molton Street, W1K 5SB
+44 (0)20 7514 0052
www.brownsfashion.com
£Affordable to expensive
10am-6:30pm

Vivienne Westwood, 44 Conduit
Street, W1S 2YJ
+44 (0)20 7439 1109
www.viviennewestwood.co.uk
£Expensive / 10am-6pm

Alexander McQueen, 4-5 Old Bond
Street, W1S 4PD
+44 (0)20 7355 0088
www.alexandermcqueen.com
£Expensive / 10am-6pm

Liberty, 210-220 Regent Street,
W1B 5AH / +44 (0)20 7734 1234
www.liberty.co.uk / £Expensive
10am-7pm M-St, 12-6pm Sn

2 Mayfair / Soho

BBC Shop, 50 Margaret Street, W1W 8SF / +44 (0)20 7631 4523 www.bbcshop.com / 9:30-6pm; 10am-5:30pm St; 12-5pm Sn

Jimmy Choo, 18 Connaught Street, W2 2AF / +44 (0)20 7262 6888 www.jimmychoo.com
£Very expensive / by appt.

Fortnum & Mason, St. James's Restaurant, 181 Piccadilly, W1A 1ER +44 (0)20 7734 8040 x2241 www.fortnumandmason.com / £20 tea 3-5:30pm

Pierre Victoire, 5 Dean Street, W1D 3RQ / +44 (0)20 7287 4582 / £20 noon-11pm; set menu to 7

Jazz at Pizza Express, 10 Dean Street, W1V 5RL +44 (0)20 7437 9595 www.pizzaexpress.co.uk/jazzsoho £20 / 11:30am-midnight; concerts 9pm, book +44 (0)20 7439 8722

The Ivy, 1 West Street, WC2H 9NQ +44 (0)20 7836 4751 www.caprice-holdings.co.uk / £40 noon-3pm, 5:30pm-midnight

Official London Theatre / tkts, Leicester Square, WC2H 7LH www.officiallondontheatre.co.uk/tkts £Half-price day-of theater tickets 10am-7pm M-St, 12-3pm Sn

W'Sens, 12 Waterloo Place, SW1Y 4AU / +44 (0)20 7484 1355 www.wsens.co.uk
£8 cocktails, £45 dinner / 7-11pm

Tiger Tiger, 29 Haymarket, SW1Y 4SP / +44 (0)20 7930 1885 www.tiger-tiger.co.uk / £10 cover noon-3am

On Anon, the London Pavilion, Piccadilly Circus, W1V 9LA +44 (0)20 7287 8008 www.onanon.co.uk / £10 cover noon-1:30am M-W, to 3am Th-St

Paragon Lounge, 9 Hanover Street, W1S 1YF / +44 (0)20 7355 3337 www.paragonlounge.co.uk
£15 cover / midnight-6am M-St; from 10pm F

Fiesta Havana, 17, Hanover Square, W1S 1HS / +44 (0)20 7629 2552 www.fiestahavana.com / £2-10 5pm-3am F-St; to 2am T-T; to 12:30am Sn-M

The Loop, 19, Dering St, W1S 1AJ +44 (0)20 7493 1003 www.theloopbar.co.uk / £10 cover 5pm-3am Th-St, noon-11pm M-W

Waxy O'Conners, 14-16 Rupert St, W1V 7FN / +44 (0)20 7287 0255 noon-11pm

Covent Garden / Strand 3

COORDINATES

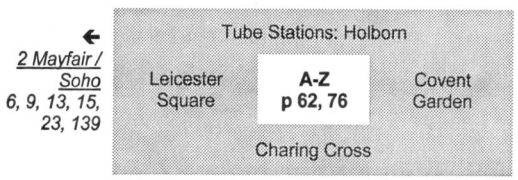

↑ *11 Bloomsbury / Clerkenwell*
Buses: 59, 68, 91, 168, 188, 243, 341

↑N

← *2 Mayfair / Soho*
6, 9, 13, 15, 23, 139

Tube Stations: Holborn

| Leicester Square | **A-Z** **p 62, 76** | Covent Garden |

Charing Cross

→ *4 Holborn*
4, 11, 23, 26, 76, 172, 521

↓ *4 Embankment*
Walk

PROFILE

Special Dates	Day				Night			
	See	Shop	Stroll	Relax	Watch	Eat	Party	Unwind
					✓			

DOSSIER

Go:	Weekday and weekend evenings for entertainment
Recognize:	Andrew Lloyd Webber, and Eliza Doolittle
Expect:	Crowds, noise, rip offs, queues, bad souvenirs, pickpockets
Wear:	Classy to the opera or a show
Avoid:	Wasting time here; bad food
Know:	Covent Garden has become so tourist-ized and commercialized that the charm it must once have had is smothered under an almost theme-park-like atmosphere. That said, the Royal Opera House is home to top-notch opera and ballet, and Theatreland extends onto Strand and Drury Lane, so world-class entertainment is always on tap.

3 Covent Garden / Strand

In the morning:
If you plan on taking in a Theatreland show, be sure to arrive at the **tkts** half-price booth at Leicester Square at 9:45 am sharp to try to score a bargain. Remember, this is for unsold tickets, so if you have your heart set on a particular show or time, it is better to book well in advance. Hot limited-run productions often sell out, especially when the big names are on stage. See what's on at the **Official London Theatre** website, www.officiallondontheatre.co.uk

In the afternoon:
Bargain hunters for the Opera or Ballet should arrive at the Royal Opera House box office at 3:45 pm. Unsold tickets for performances that evening may be made available at significant discounts at 4 pm.

For dinner:
Here's another neighborhood where a trusted recommendation is critical, since bad food abounds. Dependable chain **Pizza Express** is on Strand across the street from Charing Cross station. For charming ambiance, make reservations at **Giovanni's**, a tricky-to-find Italian joint down a tiny alleyway called Goodwin's Court, found through a little awning heading east off of St. Martin's Lane. Alternatively, those attending the opera should consider dining at one of the several fine restaurants at the Opera House.

In the evening:
An evening at the **Royal Opera House**, for either the opera or the ballet, is a luxurious treat. The building has undergone loving renovation, and the direction, sets, and costumes are exquisite, plus the talent is nearly unparalleled in the world.

Theatreland extends from the south end of Soho into Covent Garden and the Strand, with some of London's most famous theaters found on Drury Lane. London continues to be a capital of the world stage and seeing at least one show while visiting is a must.

Covent Garden / Strand

A sparkling approach to Covent Garden at night is across the Waterloo Bridge, which affords an unobstructed view of most London landmarks, romantically lit.

Those looking to tear it up on the dance floor in the later hours can head west and north to Soho and Fitzrovia. For a big name alternative check out one of the behemoths of the gay London night scene, **Heaven**, in the tunnel behind Charing Cross station, for several floors of fantastic beats and quintessential club atmosphere. Nearby Leicester Square is peppered with late-night dance halls and is a great place to hear canned music, be accosted by drunken tourists, and have your pocket picked.

Index:

- All times are daily unless noted otherwise, and are subject to change.
- Obtaining a reservation or place on the guest list is always recommended.

Official London Theatre / tkts, Leicester Square, WC2H 7LH
www.officiallondontheatre.co.uk/tkts
£ Half-price day-of theater tickets
10am-7pm M-St, 12-3pm Sn

Pizza Express, 450 Strand, WC2R 0RG / +44 (0)20 7930 8205 / £15
11:30am-midnight; to 11:30pm Sn

Giovanni's, 10 Goodwins Court, WC2N 4LL / +44 (0)20 7240 2877
£20 / noon-2:30pm, 5:30-11:30pm M-St

Royal Opera House, Bow Street, Covent Garden, WC2E 9DD
+44 (0)20 7304 4000
www.royalopera.org / £5-200
Daytime tours, evening performances Half-price tickets at the box office four hours before show time

Heaven, The Arches, Villiers Street, WC2N 6NG / +44 (0)20 7930 2020
www.heaven-london.com / £2-20
10pm-3am M, W, F; to 5am St

4 Holborn / Embankment

COORDINATES

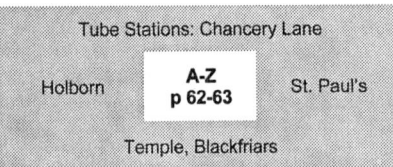

↑ *11 Bloomsbury / Clerkenwell*
Buses: 17, 45, 46

↑N

← *3 Covent Garden*
4, 11, 23, 26, 76, 172, 521

Tube Stations: Chancery Lane

Holborn   **A-Z p 62-63**   St. Paul's

Temple, Blackfriars

→ *5 City*
11, 15, 17, 23, 26, 76, 100, 388

↓ *6 Southwark / Lambeth*
17, 45, 63, 100

PROFILE

Special Dates	Day				Night			
Sept: Great River Race. Dragon boats, cutters, and other boats race to Tower. www.greatriverrace.co.uk	See	Shop	Stroll	Relax	Watch	Eat	Party	Unwind
	✓		✓					

DOSSIER

Go:	Weekdays for comparatively laid-back sightseeing
Recognize:	St. Paul's Cathedral and Courts of Justice
Expect:	Lawyers, law students, suits, tourists
Wear:	Smart, simple, comfortable for walking; a suit to blend in
Avoid:	-
Know:	"Legal London" is frequently overlooked by visitors, but it shouldn't be. Seeing the barristers in their powdered wigs is a piece of living London history. The area is home to many of Sir Christopher Wren's lovely churches (including his *piece de resistance*, St. Paul's), and breathing space is found strolling the Thames or the greens of several law schools (or "Inns") in the neighborhood.

Holborn / Embankment 4

In the morning:
Start the day at 10a.m. at **Somerset House**, a stunning 18th century building right on the Thames that houses several uniquely interesting art collections. The **Courtauld Institute of Art Gallery** is a must for Manet groupies and other Impressionist lovers. The **Gilbert Collection** is an excellent gallery of decorative and usable art from the 18th and 19th centuries. Finally, the **Hermitage Rooms,** which unusually recreate the State Hermitage Museum of St. Petersburg, Russia, also host a variety of rotating collections on loan from that institution. The three galleries can be accessed either individually or jointly for a discount.

An alternative for packrats is the **Sir John Soane Museum**, a rather overwhelming amalgamation of curios housed in the former residence of the architect, who redid the building especially to show off his extensive collection.

For lunch:
Somerset House offers several cafes and restaurants, particularly pleasant during nice weather when they feature outdoor seating. Alternatively, both High Holborn and Fleet Street are home to London's dependable chains **EAT** and **Pret a Manger**.

In the afternoon:
Church votaries will enjoy the free one o'clock concerts at two of Holborn's most lovely churches: **St. Mary-le-Strand**, sitting right in the center of the road, and **St. Brides,** with its tiered spire purportedly inspiring the now-traditional wedding cake. Performance days vary, so check the websites in advance.

Legal eagles and scandal seekers will definitely not want to skip the Central Criminal Court (a.k.a. **Old Bailey**), where the public is still welcome to watch the barristers clad in powdered wigs trying and defending the accused from 2-5 pm. Importantly, visitors may bring no mobiles, no cameras, no food, no large bags, and there are no

4 Holborn / Embankment

most important cases are typically tried in the old building in courts 1 and 2, but check before visiting to see what's going on.

Anyone with even a mild taste for silver will want to check out the **London Silver Vaults**, a subterranean hive of silver merchants. It's totally surreal and the sheer volume of jewelry, art, and serving pieces boggles the mind.

Those seeking to stretch their legs can walk the picturesque Victoria Embankment pathway along the Thames from Westminster Tube to Somerset House and then saunter up the hill to **Lincoln's Inn**, one of the four Inns of Court, where you may relax on the green.

St. Paul's Cathedral, one of the two most significant churches in London, dominates the skyline. Sightseers should arrive around 1 pm to ensure a spot in either the 1:30 or 2 pm tour, which runs 90 minutes long and includes all key points of interest. Final admission is at 4 pm. The church closes to tourists in preparation for the 5 pm evensong, so if attending, worshipers must arrive at 4:30 to claim a seat for this very moving service. Special events can interrupt the usual schedule at any time of the year, so check the website in advance.

For dinner:
Take a short walk north from High Holborn up to Lamb's Conduit, where several delectable pubs and restaurants offer a much more neighborhood feel. See Bloomsbury / Clerkenwell section on p58 for more information.

In the evening:
Holborn is much livelier by day. However, an evening stroll up Fleet Street is grand, with the Courts of Justice and many churches lit up brilliantly. Stop for a pint on Fleet Street at the **Ye Olde Cheshire Cheese**, one of the largest and most venerable pubs in London.

Holborn / Embankment 4

Index:
- All times are daily unless noted otherwise, and are subject to change.
- Obtaining a reservation or place on the guest list is always recommended.

Somerset House, including the Courtauld Institute Art Gallery, the Gilbert Collection, and the Hermitage Rooms, Strand, WC2R 1LA
+44 (0)20 7836 8686
www.somerset-house.org.uk
£5 for 1, £8 for 2, £12 for all
Café, deli 10am-6pm; restaurant to 8:45pm

Sir John Soane Museum, 13 Lincoln's Inn Fields, WC2A 3BP
+44 (0)20 7405 2107
www.soane.org / £Free
10am-5pm T-St

EAT www.eatcafe.co.uk

Pret a Manger www.pret.com

St. Mary-le-Strand, Strand, WC2B 1ES / +44 (0)20 7405 1929
www.stmarylestrand.org / £Free
concerts W at 1pm; open 11am-4pm M-F; service 11am Sn

St. Brides, Fleet Street, EC4Y 8AU
+44 (0)20 7427 0133
www.stbrides.com / £Free
concerts 1pm Tu, F; services 11am, 6:30pm Sn

Central Criminal Court (Old Bailey), EC4M 7EH
+44 (0)20 7248 3277
www.cityoflondon.gov.uk → services → law & order → Central Criminal Court / £Free / Trials 10am-1pm, 2-5pm M-F

The London Silver Vaults, Chancery House, Chancery Lane, WC2A 1QS
www.thesilvervaults.com / £Free
9am5:30pm M-F, 9am-1pm St

The Inns of Court, including Lincoln's Inn, Gray's Inn, Inner Temple, and Middle Temple
www.barcounoil.org.uk

St. Paul's Cathedral, St. Paul's Churchyard, EC4M 8AD
+44 (0)20 7236 4128
www.stpauls.co.uk / £8 +£2.50 **tour**
8:30am-4pm M-St; tours at 11, 11:30am, 1:30, 2pm. Evensong 5pm M-Sn / Café 9am-5pm, 10am-5pm Sn; Restaurant 11:30am-5pm.

Ye Olde Cheshire Cheese, 145 Fleet Street, EC4A 2BU
+44 (0)20 7353 6170
www.yeoldechesirecheese.com
11:30am-11pm

5 City

COORDINATES

↑ *12 Shoreditch / Spitalfields*
Buses: 8, 25, 26, 43, 76, 141, 388

↑N

← *4 Holborn / Embankment*
11, 15, 17, 23, 26, 76, 100, 388

Tube Stations: Moorgate
St. Paul's | **A-Z p 63-64** | Aldgate
Mansion House, Cannon Street, Bank, Monument, Tower Hill

→ *N/A*

↓ *6 Southwark / Lambeth*
21, 35, 40, 43, 133, 141, 344

PROFILE

Special Dates	Day				Night			
Nov: Lord Mayor's Show. Parade and fireworks for new Lord Mayor. www.lordmayorshow.org	See	Shop	Stroll	Relax	Watch	Eat	Party	Unwind
	✓		✓					

DOSSIER

Go:	Weekdays for high-octane sightseeing
Recognize:	Tower of London, Tower Bridge, Swiss Re Building ("The Gherkin")
Expect:	Lots of tourists at the Tower; lots of suits everywhere else
Wear:	Smart, simple, comfortable for walking; a suit to blend in
Avoid:	Wandering east into Whitechapel
Know:	Second only to Westminster in terms of iconography, today the City is the financial heart of the UK, housing the stock exchange, Bank of England, as well as investors, bankers, and insurers galore. It swarms with business folk by day, but as the least residential part of London it turns pretty eerie by night. It's a popular place for "haunted" walking tours, especially since it's the oldest part of town.

In the morning:
Arrive at Tower Hill Tube at 8:45 am with pre-purchased tickets in hand for the **Tower of London**. You'll probably battle crowds anyway, but it's worth it. The Tower is an incredible piece of history, well-maintained, well-explained, and even moderately functional – since it continues to protect the crown jewels. Combination tickets with other Historic Royal Palaces (Kensington and Hampton Court) can be purchased for a discount.

For excellent views of London and classic photo ops, go to the **Tower Bridge Exhibition**, just south of the Tower within the ramparts of the Tower Bridge.

For some decompression time, proceed west to St. Dunstan's Lane to relish the serenity of the gardens, established in the ruins of **St. Dunstan-in-the-East**, a rare City green space.

Those who have already visited the Tower or who don't need the hassle should consider beginning at the **Museum of London**. History heads will appreciate this well laid-out journey from prehistory to today. This museum is active in the community and often sponsors civic projects (like youth fashion shows), so it's worth checking the website ahead of time to see if anything special will be happening. Take a breather in another welcome green space in the City – the delightful **Postman's Gardens**, situated right around the corner.

For lunch:
Throgmorton's is a toothsome and classy establishment just behind the Bank of England, with a great restaurant, deli, and pub. Otherwise, dependable London chains **Caffe Nero**, **EAT**, and **Pret a Manger** are spread throughout the area.

In the afternoon:
The City is a hectic but still agreeable place for an afternoon walk, thanks to the handsome buildings old and new. A solid

5 City

route begins east with the latest and most spectacular addition to the skyline – the Swiss Re building, known as "**The Gherkin.**" It's a work of art. Tours can be arranged in advance for serious modern architecture devotees. Other notable skyscrapers in the area include the Lloyd's Building (tallest) and Tower 42 (unusually shaped). Just west of the Lloyds Building is **Leadenhall Market**, with atmospheric wrought iron and glass enclosing the street. Continuing west, see the Bank of England, Royal Exchange, and Mansion House around an impressive 8-point intersection. Aspiring traders and monetary policy enthusiasts will want to visit the **Bank of England Museum**, which tells the story of fiat currency and ends with a simulated trading desk.

At the end of a brief detour south is the **Monument**, a pillar erected to commemorate the cataclysmic Great Fire of 1666, which wiped out 80 percent of the structures in London (and ended the plague). Climb the 311 steps to reach some good views. To the north and west is the **Guildhall**, a beautiful 15th century structure and headquarters for the Corporation of London, which governs the City to this day. If the weather is chilly, the Guildhall is a suitable place to step inside for a spell for its medieval great hall, London print collection and clock museum. From here it is a short walk north and west up to the Museum of London.

The City is also the locale for many of Sir Christopher Wren's churches, such as the most famous and divine **St. Mary-le-Bow**, whose peals dictate who's a real Cockney (one born within earshot). Check the website for concert and service schedules.

In the evening:
Once the workday ends, the City empties. Consider taking a quick trip northeast to Brick Lane for a tasty curry at one of the many Indian restaurants located there. Continuing north brings you to Shoreditch, the hot new London night scene epicenter. See the section on Shoreditch / Spitalfields for more information.

Index:
- All times are daily unless noted otherwise, and are subject to change.
- Obtaining a reservation or place on the guest list is always recommended.

Tower of London, EC3N 4AB
+44 (0)870 756 6060
www.hrp.org.uk / £13.50, £14.50 at the gate, £11 as part of joint ticket
9am-6pm Tu-St, 10am-6pm Sn-M

Tower Bridge Exhibition, Tower Bridge, SE1 2UP
+44 (0)20 77403 3761
www.toweroflondon.org.uk / £5.50
10am-6:30pm (can vary by season)

St. Dunstan-in-the-East, St. Dunstan's Lane, EC4

Museum of London, London Wall, EC2Y 5HN / +44 (0)870 444 3852
www.museumoflondon.org.uk /£Free
10am-5:50pm, Sn 12-5:50pm; café open to 5pm

Postman's Park, King Edward Street, EC1

Caffe Nero www.caffenero.co.uk

EAT www.eatcafe.co.uk

Pret a Manger www.pret.com

Swiss Re Building (The Gherkin), 30 St. Mary Axe, EC3A 5AA
+44 (0)20 7071 5023
www.30stmaryaxe.com / £250 for a group of 8 / 10am-12, 2:30-4pm, M-F

Leadenhall Market, Gracechurch Street, EC3
www.cityoflondon.gov.uk → Our Services → Markets → Leadenhall
7am-4pm, M-F

Bank of England Museum, Threadneedle Street, EC2R 8AH
+44 (0)20 7601 5545
www.bankofengland.co.uk/museum
£Free / 10am-5pm, M-F

Monument, Monument Street, EC3R 8AH / +44 (0)20 7626 2717
www.toweroflondon.org.uk → Places to Visit → Monument / £2, £1 if purchased jointly with Tower Bridge
9:30am-5:30pm

Guildhall, EC2P 2EJ
+44 (0)20 7606 3030
www.cityoflondon.gov.uk → heritage → architecture → in city → Guildhall £2.50 Gallery (free Fri);
£Free Clock Museum
10am-5pm M-St

St. Mary-le-Bow, Cheapside, EC2V 6AU / +44 (0)20 7248 5139
www.stmarylebow.co.uk
£Free / Concerts Th 1pm; Prayer Service 5:45pm M-Th

6 Southwark / Lambeth

COORDINATES

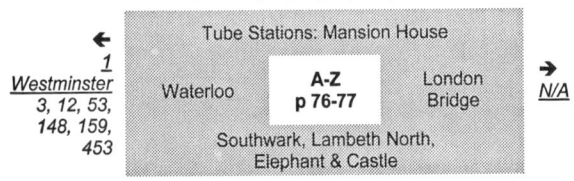

↑N

PROFILE

Special Dates	Day				Night			
	See	Shop	Stroll	Relax	Watch	Eat	Party	Unwind
Summer: Royal National Theatre Festival www.nationaltheatre.org.uk Oct/Nov: London Film Festival www.lff.org.uk	✓		✓	✓	✓		✓	✓

DOSSIER

Go:	Anytime
Recognize:	Shakespeare's Globe and London Eye
Expect:	Lots of pleasant walking, great views, surprises
Wear:	Smart, simple, comfortable for walking by day; gear up for the club scene
Avoid:	Getting lost; have your map with you
Know:	Eclectic, vibrant, and distinctly more laid-back than its better-known sister on the other side of the Thames, the South Bank provides the perfect counterpoint to the north side of the river, bringing out London's fuller flavors. Missing this neighborhood is a common visitor's mistake. Home to great art, great performances, great pubs, and great views – it's a treat.

Southwark / Lambeth

In the morning:

The **Tate Modern** joined the ranks of elite modern art museums with much fanfare in 2000, and it lives up to the hype. This enormous converted power station is perfectly suited to showing off the unusual works of the 20th century. A scenic approach is from St. Paul's, down the hill and across the pedestrian Millennium Bridge.

Those who have already visited the TM or just don't dig modern may want to instead begin the day in Lambeth. From Westminster Tube, stroll through the picturesque Victoria Tower Gardens and across Lambeth Bridge to **Lambeth Palace**, seat of the Archbishop of Canterbury since the 12th century. Access to this medieval complex is rare – those interested should enquire well ahead of their trip about a private tour. Anyone can visit London's first public library in the beautifully restored crypt and Great Hall.

Next door in St. Mary-at-Lambeth Church is the **Museum of Garden History**, a delight for green thumbs with a lovely garden out back. Through the Archbishop's Park is another quirky find – the **Florence Nightingale Museum**, depicting the crusade of the enterprising nurse against germs. History and military aficionados should advance east to the **Imperial War Museum**. Blunt, moving, rich, raw – this museum holds nothing back in its honest depiction of the heroism and tyranny of warfare.

For lunch:

The Tate Modern provides both a café and restaurant with a view of the Thames and the skyline, featuring St. Paul's. Pubs and cafes line the river, or enjoy the view with succulent picnic tidbits available at the **Borough Market -** best on Friday or Saturday when at its liveliest. This recently rejuvenated market is where London's top restaurants get their daily specials at 3 am.

6 Southwark / Lambeth

In the afternoon:
The South Bank is home to some bizarre residents[1]. The **Saatchi Gallery,** renowned for showcasing cutting-edge, envelope-pushing contemporary art, such as sculptures made of corpses or a room full of flies, is usually an olfactory as well as visual experience. Surrealism fiends may want to visit the Dalí Universe, but although it is an extensive collection many of his best works remain at other museums around the world. Finally, cuppa cognoscente shouldn't miss the **Bramah Museum of Tea and Coffee** for the histories of these behemoth world commodities. Stay for afternoon tea and crumpets.

Especially on a nice day, this is a perfect part of town for a leisurely pub-crawl and stroll along the Queen's walk, stretching nearly the entirety of this bank of the Thames. It's a fine place to wander, but the place to start is the **George Inn,** just south of London Bridge, London's only surviving galleried coaching inn, visited by both Chaucer and Dickens. Choose from several popular stops on the river flanking both sides of the Tate, including the charming **Market Porter** on the west side of the Borough Market. Intrepid crawlers may wish to venture farther inland to super sleek **Baltic**, which has tasty fare and a stunning array of vodkas, or the **Royal Oak**, a supremely welcoming old-fashioned pub to settle in for the night with pint in hand. Cheers!

For dinner:
A laid-back pub dinner could easily be in order at any of the many pubs along the river. However, those looking for more class should go to the **Oxo Tower** restaurant for a pricey first-class meal, the brasserie for a (slightly) more wallet-friendly alternative, or the bar for a G&T and a bar meal with a view.

---

[1] Two oddities which are wildly popular with tourists are the Clink Prison Exhibit and the London Dungeon. For a more realistic look at debtors' fates, visit the Foundling Museum. www.foundlingmuseum.org.uk

Southwark / Lambeth

In the evening:

A flight on the **London Eye** at sunset, when the city is stunningly illuminated, is a treat. Booking tickets ahead of time (min. 14 hours) is essential, but it's also wise to wait for the weather report, since on a rainy day it loses 90 percent of its appeal. Be sure to show up about 45 minutes ahead of time to collect your tickets and board[1].

From May to October, a performance at **Shakespeare's Globe Theater** presents the real thing, magical and unforgettable. Often, the lesser-known the play, the higher the quality of the performance. Those taking advantage of the £5 bargain standing-room ("Groundling") tickets in the Yard *must* be at the doors as they open to claim a space against the rails at the back (having the wall to lean on for a couple of hours significantly improves the quality of the experience). The Globe does not offer discounts on returned tickets, so book as far in advance as possible – everything sells out.

However, the Globe hardly has a monopoly on the Bard. The nearby **Royal National Theatre** puts on a stunning array of theatrical productions, including sublime renditions of Shakespearean works.

A multi-faceted entertainment alternative is **Royal Festival Hall**, home to the world-class London Symphony Orchestra and regular exhibitor of superb musical performers from all over the globe. It boasts a great view and a good café for a convenient pre-performance dining option.

For the high-voltage London night scene hit the **Ministry of Sound**, a dance institution. If you were even thinking about showing up in

---

[1] A popular attraction in the same riverside building as the ticket office is the London Aquarium. Wait until you get the chance to visit Underwater World in Singapore. www.underwaterworld.com.sg

6 Southwark / Lambeth

jeans and a T don't neglect to shop at Camden Market for hip and funky clubbing threads before you go.

Index:
- All times are daily unless noted otherwise, and are subject to change.
- Obtaining a reservation or place on the guest list is always recommended.

Tate Modern, Bankside, SE1 9TG
+44 (0)20 7887 8000
www.tate.org.uk / £Free / 10am-6pm Sn-Th, to 10pm F-St / café, restaurant same hours

Lambeth Palace, Lambeth Palace Rd, SE1 7JU / +44 (0)20 7898 1200
www.archbishopofcanterbury.org
Call well in advance for info

Lambeth Palace Library, Lambeth Palace Rd, SE1 7JU
+44 (0)20 7898 1400
www.lambethpalacelibrary.org
£Free / 10am-5pm M-F

Museum of Garden History, St. Mary-at-Lambeth, Lambeth Palace Rd, SE1 7LB / +44 (0)20 7401 8865
www.cix.co.uk/~museumgh/ / £3
10:30am-5pm / café same hours

Florence Nightingale Museum, 2 Lambeth Palace Road SE1 7EW
+44 (0) 20 7620 0374
www.florence-nightingale.co.uk / £6
10am-5pm, to 4:30pm St-Sn

Imperial War Museum, Lambeth Road, London SE1 6HZ
+44 (0)20 7416 5000
www.iwm.org.uk / £Free / 10am-6pm
café

Borough Market, 8 Southwark Street, SE1 1TL
+44 (0)20 7407 1002
www.boroughmarket.org.uk / £Free
12-6pm F, 9am-4pm St

Saatchi Gallery, County Hall, South Bank, SE17PB / +44 (0)20 7823 2363 www.saatchi-gallery.co.uk / £9
10am-8pm Sn-Th, 10am-10pm F-St

Bramah Museum of Tea and Coffee, 40 Southwark Street, SE1 1UN / +44 (0)20 7403 5650
www.bramahmuseum.co.uk / £4
10am-6pm / Tea Room same hours

George Inn, 77 Borough High St, SE1 1NH / +44 (0)20 7407 2056
www.nationaltrust.org.uk / 12-11pm

Southwark / Lambeth 6

Market Porter, 9 Stoney St, SE1 9AA +44 (0)20 7407 2495 / 12-11pm

Baltic, 74 Blackfriars Road, SE1 8HA +44 (0)20 7928 1111
www.balticrestaurant.co.uk
12-11pm

Royal Oak, 44 Tabard Street, SE1 4JU / +44 (0)20 7357 7173
11:30am-11pm

Oxo Tower Restaurant, Brasserie, & Bar, Bargehouse Street, SE1 9PH +44 (0)20 7803 3888
www.oxotower.co.uk / £60 restaurant, £40 brasserie
noon-2:30pm, 6pm-11pm M-St;
noon-3pm, 6:30pm-10pm Sn

London Eye, Riverside Building, County Hall, Westminster Bridge Rd, SE1 7PB / +44 (0)870 990 8881
www.londoneye.com / £12.50
9:30am-8pm, to 9pm May-Jun, Sept;
to 10pm Jul-Aug

Shakespeare's Globe Theatre, 21 New Globe Walk, Bankside, SE1 9DT +44 (0)20 7401 9919
www.shakespeares-globe.org
£5-30 / May-Sep

Royal National Theatre, SE1 9PX +44 (0)20 7452 3000
www.nationaltheatre.org.uk / £10-40
Box Office 10am-8pm M-St; shows year round

Royal Festival Hall, Belvedere Road, SE1 8XX / +44 (0)870 401 8181 www.rfh.org.uk / £5-50
times vary, shows year round

Ministry of Sound, 103 Gaunt St, SE1 6DP / +44 (0)20 7740 8627
www.ministryofsound.com / £15
cover 10:30am-5.30pm F-St

7 Chelsea / Fulham

COORDINATES

↑ *8 Knightsbridge / South Kensington*
Buses: 14, 19, 22, 414

↑N

← *7 Fulham*
11, 14, 211, 414

Tube Stations: South Kensington

| Fulham Broadway | **A-Z** **p 87-88** | Sloane Square |

Battersea Park *(National Rail, Victoria Station)*

→ *1 Westminster*
11, 211

↓ *13 Clapham*
C3, 49, 319

PROFILE

Special Dates	Day				Night			
	See	Shop	Stroll	Relax	Watch	Eat	Party	Unwind
May: Chelsea Flower Show www.rhs.org.uk Feb: London Fashion Week www.londonfashion week.co.uk		✓	✓	✓	✓			✓

DOSSIER

Go:	Weekday shop & stroll
Recognize:	Bentleys, Aston Martins
Expect:	Quiet languid snobbery, fabulous (expensive) shopping, beautiful homes, tree-lined streets
Wear:	Subtle, expensive, stylish; wear expensive shoes and carry an expensive bag. Think Manhattan, not Beverly Hills.
Avoid:	Being in the center of the neighborhood when you're getting tired – there's practically no public transport in Chelsea.
Know:	Chelsea is the best neighborhood in London to get lost in. Quiet, picturesque, and full of luxurious shops, there are no tourist attractions and no Tube stations, so it is mercifully tourist-free.

In the morning:
A serious shopping trip in Chelsea could easily take all day, particularly if combined with Knightsbridge / Brompton / Sloane Square. Sloane Avenue (not Street) essentially forms the northern border of Chelsea as far as shopping is concerned. North of this find the big global brands like Burberry, in the south of Chelsea are the more quietly fabulous boutiques. A couple of favorites are colorful **Butler & Wilson**, with excellent accessories downstairs and a breathtaking vintage section upstairs, and **Courtezan**, which is more like a trip into *Liasons Dangerouse* than a clothier. Both Fulham Road and King's Road from Sloane Square west are strewn with shops. Figure £300 shoes, £250 jeans, £200 tops.

Chelsea is a brilliant place to browse, but it is much more spread out than Mayfair, so if seeking something specific be sure to pick up a copy of *Time Out Shopping* guide or *Wear to Where* for more guidance on details. Anyone with limited time to wander should focus on the triangle defined by Sloane Square, South Kensington Tube, and Sydney Street.

For lunch:
If in the area of Sloane Square, consider the **Fox & Hounds**, a delightful pub with excellent fare. If in the far western reaches of Chelsea, go to **The Troubadour**, a flavorsome café famous for its eclectic décor and history as a performing venue (Hendrix, Dylan, Simon, etc.). However, the restaurant worth a walk is **Bibendum**, one of the bastions of Sir Terence Conran, a living culinary legend. It delivers because of its fantastic digs in the renovated art deco Michelin Tire building (on top of award-winning food and wine). The more casual café serves as an alternative to the pricey restaurant.

In the afternoon:
It would be easy to continue shopping for the rest of the day, however, those fortunate enough to be in Chelsea on a Wednesday or Sunday afternoon from April to October should make their way to

7 Chelsea / Fulham

the magical **Chelsea Physic Garden**. This tenderly maintained living link to medical history is aptly called London's "secret garden." Those wishing for access to the garden at any time can become a Friend of the Garden online for £15 with unlimited access. For some wide-open green space, consider crossing the attractive Albert Bridge to **Battersea Park.** Up until very recently one of London's best-kept secrets, it's coming up in the world now as home to London Fashion Week. The park is a true community park with lots of sport facilities, an art gallery, a children's zoo, and things of that like. But don't forget that simply wandering is a splendid way to spend the afternoon in Chelsea!

For dinner:
It's hard to go far astray. There are a number of restaurants to choose from around the bend on Brompton Road. Those who missed **Bibendum** at lunch may want to rectify that at dinner. Those planning on a night out on-the-town may prefer to focus on the area at Fulham Broadway, where there are many good and relatively cheap restaurants and pubs. Another option for a splurge is **Blue Elephant** which features tempting food and fun Thai jungle décor.

In the evening:
Real football fans, sport devotees and hottie addicts will want to buy tickets to a **Chelsea F.C.** home match the minute after their flight is booked. Nothing in England compares to the fire and fury of football (what we call "soccer"). Perhaps a Red Sox/Yankees playoff game comes close back home. Do not wear the opposing team's colors and do not cop an attitude. Spectators are regularly harmed at football matches for acting like idiots – so don't.

Those seeking a fun, young, and relaxed pub/bar crawl might head west to Fulham Broadway for a variety of destinations. The **Fiesta Havana,** a chilled-out version of its Mayfair sister, regularly serves up live music. Pub **Bootsy Brogan's** often has a friendly,

Chelsea / Fulham

boisterous crowd. Nearby pedestrian-friendly Jerdan Place and Farm Close are worth checking out. Live music junkies will instead want to have a look at the schedule of The Club at The Troubadour, who put on both big name and new artist sessions.

Butler & Wilson, 189 Fulham Road, SW3 6JN / +44 (0)20 7352 3045
www.butlerandwilson.co.uk
Moderate / 10am-6pm, to 7pm W, 12-6pm Sn

Courtezan, 84 Fulham Road, SW3 6HR / +44 (0)20 7584 0044
Expensive / 10am-6pm M-Sn

Fox & Hounds, 29 Passmore St, SW1W 8HR / +44 (0)20 7730 6367
11am–11pm

The Troubadour, 263-7 Old Brompton Road, SW5 9JA
+44 (0)20 7370 1434
www.troubadour.co.uk / 11am-11pm, can be later on weekends

Bibendum, 81 Fulham Road, SW3 6RD / +44 (0)20 7581 5817
www.bibendum.co.uk
£35 lun, £60 din; £10 café
noon-2pm, 7-11pm M-F; 12:30-2:30pm, 7-10:30pm St-Sn

Chelsea Physic Garden, 66 Royal Hospital Road, SW3 4HS
+44 (0)20 7352 5646
www.chelseaphysicgarden.co.uk
£6 / 2-6pm Sn, 12-5pm W Apr-Oct; unlimited access for £15

Battersea Park, SW11 4NJ
www.batterseapark.org / 8am-dusk

Blue Elephant, 4-6 Fulham Broadway, SW6 1AA
+44 (0)20 7385 6595
www.blueelephant.com/london
£45 / noon-2:30pm, 7pm-midnight

Chelsea F.C., Stamford Bridge, Fulham Road, SW6 1HS
+44 (0)20 7386 9383
www.chelseafc.com
Box Office 9am-5pm M-F

Fiesta Havana, 490 Fulham Road, SW6 5 NH / +44 (0)20 7381 5005
www.fiestahavana.com / £3-8 cover after 9pm / 5pm-2am

Bootsy Brogan's, 1 Fulham Broadway, SW6 1AA
+44 (0)20 7385 2003
www.brogansfulham.co.uk / 11am-11pm; to midnight Th, Sn; to 1am F

8 Knightsbridge / South Kensington

COORDINATES

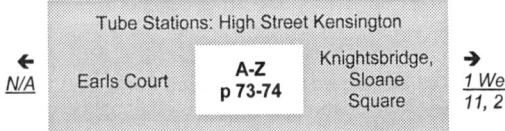

↑ *8 Holland Park / Notting Hill*
Buses: 28, 70, 328

↑**N**

←				→
N/A	Earls Court	Tube Stations: High Street Kensington **A-Z** **p 73-74** South Kensington	Knightsbridge, Sloane Square	*1 Westminster* 11, 211

↓ *7 Chelsea*
14, 19, 22, 414

PROFILE

Special Dates	Day				Night			
Jan/Jul: clothing sales Sept: Proms Last Night www.royalalberthall.com Sept: Street Fashion Auction www.christies.com	See	Shop	Stroll	Relax	Watch	Eat	Party	Unwind
	✓	✓	✓	✓	✓	✓	✓	

DOSSIER

Go:	Weekday sightseeing, shopping; weekend night glam clubbing
Recognize:	Harrods and designer labels
Expect:	In-your-face snobbery, fabulous (expensive) shopping, label whores, crowds, noise
Wear:	Labels. Wear expensive sunglasses and carry an expensive bag. Think Paris Hilton.
Avoid:	Getting lost in Harrods
Know:	Sport your designer threads here and come prepared to drop some change on more. It's more than just shopping, though – Knightsbridge is home to top museums, parks, and performance venues, too.

Knightsbridge / South Kensington 8

In the morning:
The Victoria & Albert Museum (better known as the **V&A**) is a temple to decorative arts (including fashion) housed in a gorgeous building and named London's top attraction in 2004. While undergoing massive renovations until 2007, various parts of the museum will be closed off, but the sheer size of the collections makes this a non-issue. It is recommended to arrive as the museum opens at 10 am to mitigate the impact of crowds on your visit.

Those who have already visited the V&A may consider a stop at the nearby Science and Natural History Museums, also housed in lovely buildings and originally part of the V&A. These museums do have extensive collections, but adult visitors should be aware that they are set up primarily with children in mind.

For lunch:
The V&A has several good cafes and a restaurant, although these can become prohibitively crowded on a busy day. For shoppers *the* place to have lunch is the 5th Floor restaurant at Harvey Nichols (better known as **Harvey Nicks**). Those not wanting to pay through the nose for lunch can have a lighter meal at the HN café.

In the afternoon:
Designer shopping is the top Knightsbridge afternoon activity. High-end department store Harvey Nichols is a superb place to start, followed by a visit to the **Burberry** flagship store across the street. West down Brompton Road, encounter many outstanding shops, including the unmistakable Harrods[1]. Several streets further on is Beauchamp Place, home to **Bertie Golightly**, a second-hand clothier *par excellence* and worth checking for a steal. Curving back east to Sloane Street brings you to **Lulu Guinness**, a handbag

---

[1] Harrods' exterior is beautifully illuminated at night. Its interior has nearly become too crowded for its own good. For a beautiful afternoon tea consider Fortnum & Mason.

8 Knightsbridge / South Kensington

legend in her own time. Die-hard (and wealthy) fashionistas may desire an appointment at **Manolo Blahnik**.

On a sunny day it would be a crime to miss **Hyde Park** and **Kensington Gardens**, central London's source of oxygen and R&R. Stroll, sit, people-watch, see some art, watch some sports, hear some music, enjoy some kids, feed the swans. However, the top attraction may be afternoon tea at **The Orangery**, just across the sunken garden from **Kensington Palace** at the far west end of the park. Once a specialized greenhouse for citrus trees, it is now a bright, light and cheery setting for an absolutely English afternoon indulgence. The Palace itself is an interesting place to visit, particularly for anyone curious about ceremonial court dress.

For dinner:
A meal at the classy and affable gastropub **The Abingdon** makes for a delicious way to while-away an evening in comfortable style. Those who have had enough snobbery may opt to cross the invisible barrier west to gritty, grimy Shepherd's Bush for a vodka-laced Polish smörgåsbord at restaurant **Patio**.

In the evening:
Royal Albert Hall, an immense performance hall designed for choral concerts, is an unusual and beautiful building with surprisingly superb acoustics. The Hall has two restaurants and a café for convenient pre-performance dining. Big name events may sell out, so check the schedule before your trip. World-famous are the summer "Proms," which feature a wide selection of music.

However, this neighborhood is better-known for its glamorous nightclubs, often the backdrops for photos of "It" girls in the gossip rags. A crawl in this neighborhood starts on Kensington Church Street and then doglegs east to Kensington Gore. Cocktail aficionados should return to Beauchamp Place where you'll be spoiled for choice at **Townhouse**.

Knightsbridge / South Kensington 8

Index:
- All times are daily unless noted otherwise, and are subject to change.
- Obtaining a reservation or place on the guest list is always recommended.

V&A (Victoria & Albert Museum), Cromwell Road, SW7 2RL
+44 (0)20 7942 2000
www.vam.ac.uk / £Free
10am-5:45pm, to 10pm W

Harvey Nicks (Harvey Nichols), 109-125 Knightsbridge, SW1X 7RJ
+44 (0)20 7235 5000
www.harveynichols.com
Expensive / lunch from 12-3pm at the restaurant, café open all day

Burberry, 2 Brompton Road, SW1X 7PB / +44 (0)20 7581 2151
www.burberry.com / £Expensive
10am-7pmM-St; noon-6pm Sn

Bertie Golightly, 48 Beauchamp Place, SW3 1NX
+44 (0)20 7584 7270
www.bertiego.co.uk / £Moderate to expensive / 10am-6pm, 12-5pm Sn

Lulu Guinness, 3 Ellis Street, SW1X 9AL / +44 (0)20 7823 4828
www.luluguinness.com / £Expensive
10am-6pm; 11am-6pm St; closed Sn

Manolo Blahnik, 49-51 Old Church Street, SW3 5BS
+44 (0)20 7352 3863 / £Very Expensive / 10am-5:30pm; 10:30am-5pm St; closed Sn

Hyde Park /www.royalparks.gov.uk

Kensington Gardens
www.royalparks.gov.uk / 6am-dusk

The Orangery Tea Rooms, Kensington Gardens, W8 4PX
+44 (0)20 7376 0239
www.hrp.org.uk → Kensington Palace → Visit → Eating / £15
10am-6pm

Kensington Palace, Kensington Gardens, W8 4PX
+44 (0)870 751 5180
www.hrp.org.uk / £11 (£10 online, £9 w/ Tower) / 10am-6pm

The Abingdon, 54 Abingdon Road, W0 6AP / +44 (0)20 7937 3339
£25 / 12:30-2:30pm, 6:30-11pm M-F; to 3pm St, Sn; din 7-10pm Sn

Patio, 5 Goldhawk Road, W12 8QQ
+44 (0)20 8743 5194 / £20 / noon-3pm M-F; 6pm-11:30pm M-Sn

Royal Albert Hall, Kensington Gore, SW7 2AP / +44 (0)20 7589 8212
www.royalalberthall.com / £15-60
restaurant, café open 2 hours before performance

Townhouse, 31 Beauchamp Place, SW3 1NU / +44 (0)20 7589 5080
www.lab-townhouse.com
4:30-11 M-F, Sn; noon-midnight St

9 Holland Park / Notting Hill

COORDINATES

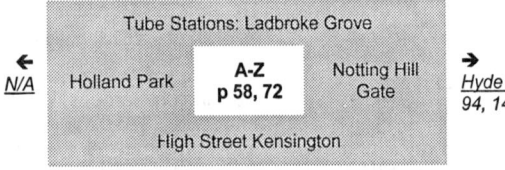

↑ *14 Hampstead / Camden Town*
Buses: 27, 31, 328

↑N

Tube Stations: Ladbroke Grove

← *N/A* Holland Park   **A-Z p 58, 72**   Notting Hill Gate → *Hyde Park* 94, 148, 390

High Street Kensington

↓ *8 Knightsbridge / South Kensington*
28, 70, 328

PROFILE

Special Dates	Day				Night			
Aug: Notting Hill Carnival www.thecarnival.tv Jun: London Garden Square Weekend http://myweb.tiscali.co.uk/	See	Shop	Stroll	Relax	Watch	Eat	Party	Unwind
		✓	✓	✓				

DOSSIER

Go:	Fridays for clothes market; Saturdays for antiques
Recognize:	A paparazzi-dodging celebrity, if you're sharp
Expect:	Good shopping, friendly atmosphere, stately homes, crowds on weekends
Wear:	Preppy trendy yuppie casual, comfortable for walking; chic for the evening
Avoid:	Leaving the core north/south corridor – there are many unattractive and/or unpleasant neighborhoods in the area.
Know:	Notting Hill and Holland Park may have achingly high opinions of themselves, but who can blame them? This place is cool. Portobello Road lives up to its reputation, Holland Park is a secret gem, and the lovely homes make for highly pleasant afternoon perambulations.

Holland Park / Notting Hill

In the morning:
Early risers may choose to start the day at **Little Venice** (Warwick Avenue Tube), a serene, pretty, and much sought-after address, to walk the canal and enjoy the enchanting canal boat homes. There are several good places around for a cup of coffee or a nice breakfast. From here it is a 20-minute jaunt west along the canal to Meanwhile Gardens, a small green space on Goldborne Road leading right onto **Portobello Road**.

This half-mile stretch of colorful shop fronts is globally famous for its Saturday morning antiques street market, where quality is high – and so are the prices. Portobello Road, however, and neighbors Westbourne Grove and Ledbury Road, are locally known for great clothes, particularly on Fridays when there is a clothes market at the **Portobello Green Arcade**, also home to outrageous rocker favorite **Debonair Debonair**. A not-so-secret celebrity hang-out is label emporium **Matches**, which doubles as a bar.

For lunch:
It's hard to go wrong in this relatively solid neighborhood for lunch with plenty of pubs, restaurants, and cafes. A respectable trendy spot is the **Electric Brasserie** right on Portobello Road.

In the afternoon:
On a nice day, a great place for a ramble is the cinnamon-roll layout of the Hill itself, full of beautiful homes and exclusive walled gardens. The tiny square at the intersection of Portland Road and Penzance Place is peaceful and charming. From there it's a short walk across Holland Park Avenue into **Holland Park**, one of central London's frequently overlooked gems. It has a sweet little café, a couple of art galleries, several different gardens, and best of all, a cricket ground where you're likely to catch a match on a weekend. It's a pleasing place for a leg stretch and people watching, to read a book or talk to a friend, and savor some refreshment and relaxation.

9 Holland Park / Notting Hill

Architects and interior designers will fancy a stop at the **Leighton House Museum** just south of the park. Lord Leighton did each room of his house in a unique period and regional style[1], which has been preserved exactly as it was on the day he died.

For dinner:
It's unlikely that any choice in this neighborhood will be a poor one. Discover several good restaurants at the south end of Portland Road, including perpetually hip **Julie's**. A neighborhood institution is **The Cow** pub and restaurant right in the thick of things.

In the evening:
During the summer Holland Park is the setting of sublime outdoor opera. Picnics tend more towards champagne and caviar rather than beer and hoagies. It is worthwhile purchasing tickets well in advance.

The nightlife in this neighborhood bleeds into the scene on Kensington Church Street and southward. However, the **Notting Hill Arts Club,** well-known for its cozy atmosphere and great DJs, is a suitable place to kick off the evening (and maybe finish it too!). Futuristic and exclusive **Lonsdale** will make you feel like one of the who's who. Chic and stylish 19th century **Elgin** is probably the hippest listed pub in London.

---

[1] Fanatical design devotees will want to make the trek to the Geffrye Museum in Hoxton, north of Shoreditch. It's in the middle of nowhere in a seedy neighborhood, but it chronicles interior design from 1600 to the present day in several beautifully restored Georgian homes. Modern exhibitions, a garden, and restaurant complete the experience.
www.geffrye-museum.org.uk

Holland Park / Notting Hill 9

Index:
- All times are daily unless noted otherwise, and are subject to change.
- Obtaining a reservation or place on the guest list is always recommended.

Portobello Market
www.portobelloroad.co.uk / Saturday

Portobello Green Arcade, 281 Portobello Road W10 5TZ

Debonair Debonair, Portobello Green Arcade, W10 5TZ
+44 (0)20 8960 7679 / £Moderate to expensive
10:30am-6pm; closed Sn

Matches, 60-64 Ledbury Road, W11 2AJ / +44 (0)20 8944 7820
www.matches.co.uk / £Very expensive / 10am-6pm; 12-6pm Sn

Electric Brasserie, 191 Portobello Road, W11 2ED
+44 (0)20 7908 9696
www.electricbrasserie.com / £15
8am-11pm

Holland Park / www.rbkc.gov.uk → Local life → Parks / Opera Box Office +44 (0)845 230 9769 / £20-60

Leighton House Museum, 12 Holland Park Road, W14 8LZ
+44 (0)20 7602 3316
www.rbkc.gov.uk → Local life → Arts & Museums / £3
11am-5:30pm; closed Tu

Julie's, 135 Portland Road, W11 4LW / +44 (0)20 7229 8331
www.juliesrestaurant.com / £45
noon-11:30pm

The Cow Saloon Bar & Dining Rooms, 89 Westbourne Park Road, W2 5QH / +44 (0)20 7221 0021 /£15
bar 24-7; dining noon-3pm, 6-10:30pm

Notting Hill Arts Club, 21 Notting Hill Gate, W11 3JQ
+44 (0)20 7460 4459
www.nottinghillartsclub / £Free-8
6pm-1am; to 2am Th-F; 4pm-2am St, 4pm-12:30am Sn

Lonsdale, 44-48 Lonsdale Road, W11 2DE / +44 (0)20 7228 1517
www.thelonsdale.co.uk
6pm-midnight M-St; 6-11:30pm Sn

Elgin, 96 Ladbroke Grove, W11 1PY
+44 (0)20 7229 5663
11am-11pm M-St; noon-10:30pm Sn

10 Marylebone / Fitzrovia

COORDINATES

↑N

↑ *14 Hampstead / Camden Town*
Buses: 27, 274

← *Little Venice* 6, 414

Baker Street

Tube Stations: Regent's Park, Great Portland Street

A-Z p 60, 61

Warren St, Goodge St

Bond Street, Oxford Circus, Tottenham Court Road

→ *11 Bloomsbury / Clerkenwell* 7

↓ *2 Mayfair / Soho*
13, 113, 139, 189, 453

PROFILE

Special Dates	Day				Night			
	See	Shop	Stroll	Relax	Watch	Eat	Party	Unwind
Jun/Jul: London College of Fashion Degree Show Exhibition +44 (0)20 7514 7316	✓	✓	✓	✓	✓	✓	✓	

DOSSIER

Go:	Anytime
Recognize:	The London of Doyle and Dickens
Expect:	Bustle, charm, neighborhood feel
Wear:	Smart casual, comfortable for walking
Avoid:	Very busy Marylebone and Euston Roads
Know:	Marylebone is a classic village from another age, overlooked despite its location in the very heart of town. Old London in miniature, it's a wonderfully easy way to spend a day with a little bit of everything. Across the invisible barrier on Regent Street, nocturnal Fitzrovia revs into life at twilight when the college kids get out of class and the DJs set up.

Marylebone / Fitzrovia

In the morning:

The **Wallace Collection** has been referred to as "criminally overlooked" – this least-known of London's major art galleries boasts an exquisite Renaissance collection, excellent exhibitions, and a wide range of educational programs. Painting enthusiasts will not want to miss it, and anyone intimidated by the frequent crush of visitors at other museums will enjoy the relative quiet at the WC[1].

Those interested in undiscovered contemporary art will want to visit the small but spunky **A&D Gallery**, brainchild of architects Andy and Danny who grew tired of other galleries refusing to show their designs. In the tradition of good galleries, this snub at The Man has turned into a great little business. Artists should call ahead to obtain an invite to one of the closed-list soirees A&D throw for the opening of each show.

Others seeking an indulgently relaxing day should pack their coolers and go west to the **Lord's Cricket Ground** for a test match. The "short" matches last a day – long ones last as many as five – which means that spectators get to hang out in the sun all day getting slowly toasted. For those who don't know the rules, give the website a good study ahead of time for a grasp of the game.

For lunch:

Café Bagatelle at the Wallace Collection is a pleasant and convenient choice. Those planning on shopping in Marylebone may instead want to dine at one of the several restaurants on Gees Court / St. Christopher's Place just off of Oxford Street. Another agreeable possibility is London's best lunch chain, **Giraffe**, specializing in tasty world eats and beats.

---

[1] One of the reasons for the Wallace Collection's relative anonymity is its proximity to several painfully popular London tourist attractions, namely Madame Toussaud's Wax Museum, the Planetarium, the London Zoo, and the Sherlock Holmes Museum. Long queues, astronomic cheese levels, and high prices can be expected at all four.

10 Marylebone / Fitzrovia

In the afternoon:
Marylebone is a great place to shop because of both its picturesque high street and its unusually high concentration of specialty shops housed in spectacularly maintained centuries' old buildings. Among the first-rate vendors are **The Button Queen, V V Rouleaux** (fine fabrics and ribbon), **Daunt's Books**, **Philip Somerville** (milliner to the Queen), **Biggles Sausages** and **Blagden Fishmongers**, along with a host of other classically photogenic locales.

There are many excellent clothing shops tucked away north of Oxford Street on Gees Court / St. Christopher's Place and Marylebone High Street itself has many classy, stylish stores. Bargain and vintage hunters will want to wend their way to **Catwalk** to browse for some terrific deals. Marylebone falls between Mayfair's Oxford and Bond Streets in terms of price, figure the £100-200 range for jeans, tops, shoes, and bags.

The jewel of Marylebone is green and airy **Regent's Park**. It would be easy to spend a whole day here, between the beautiful Queen Mary's Gardens, the boating lake, the newly refurbished sport fields, miles of trails, and the open-air theater (which does Shakespeare under the stars in the summer). Just north stands **Primrose Hill** – one of few public places with a sweeping panoramic view of London.

For dinner:
A warm, elegant and romantic option is French **Orrery**, right at the top of Marylebone High Street. **Providores,** a successful fusion cuisine experiment by Kiwi Peter Gordon, provides both a laid-back tapas bar and more formal restaurant. It's hard to go wrong with any of the options along the high street or down Marylebone Lane. Those attending an evening concert at Wigmore Hall will dine well and conveniently at their newly refurbished bar or restaurant.

Marylebone / Fitzrovia 10

The nightlife in Fitzrovia can easily be accompanied by one of the many restaurants on Mortimer, Great Titchfield, and Charlotte Streets, for those who would like to bar-hop and food browse simultaneously. A local favorite is Sardinian **Sardo**, welcoming and very tasty.

In the evening:

Chamber music gluttons need look no further than the delicious *fin-de-siècle* **Wigmore Hall**. Great performers usually only heard in front of a world-class symphony orchestra grant chamber performances in this intimate and acoustically perfect setting.

Dusk, in Marylebone, is a fresh and flirty starter to a cocktail kind of night, but college-crowd Fitzrovia is the real place for a power bar crawl. To the north on Cleveland Street are various bars, including **Southside** with an incredible cocktail menu, plus treats and lollies from the Antipodes. Centrally located **Nordic** introduces more international flavor with plenty of vodka and a serious (and cheap!) smörgåsbord. To the south lies the **Marquis of Granby,** a lively pub at the intersection of Rathbone Street and Rathbone Place. In between are plenty of selections for drinking and dancing. Cheers!

Wallace Collection, Hartford House, Manchester Square, W1U 3BN / +44 (0)20 7563 9500
www.wallacecollection.org / £Free
10am-5pm / Café same hours

A&D Gallery, 51 Chiltern St, W1U 6LY / +44 (0)20 7486 0534
www.a-and-d.co.uk / £Free
10:30am–7pm

Lord's Cricket Ground, St. John's Wood Road, NW8 8QN
+44 (0)20 7432 1000 /
www.lords.org/ £5-50

Giraffe, 6-8 Blandford Street, W1U 4AU / +44 (0)20 935 2333
www.giraffe.net / £10
8am-11pm; from 9am on St-Sn

The Button Queen, 19 Marylebone Lane, W1U 2NF
+44 (0)20 7935 1505
www.thebuttonqueen.co.uk
10am-5pm; 10am-6pm Th-F; 10am-4pm St; closed Sn

Phillip Somerville, 38 Chiltern Street, W1U 7QL
+44 (0)20 7224 1517
9am-5:30pm M-F

10 Marylebone / Fitzrovia

V V Rouleaux, 6 Marylebone High Street, W1M 3PB
+44 (0)20 7224 5179
www.vvrouleaux.com / 9:30am-6pm M-St; from 10:30am on W

Daunt Books, 83 Marylebone High Street, W1U 4QW
+44 (0)20 7224 2295
www.dauntbooks.co.uk
9am-7:30pm; 11am-6pm Sn

Biggles Gourmet Sausages, 66 Marylebone Lane, W1U 2NU
+44 (0)20 7224 5937
www.ebiggles.co.uk / 10am-6pm; 10am-4:30pm Sn-M

Blagden Fishmongers, 65 Paddington Street, W1U 4JQ
+44 (0)20 7935 8321 / 7:30am-5pm; 7:30am-1pm M, St; closed Sn

Catwalk, 52 Blandford Street, W1U 7HT / +44 (0)20 7935 1052
£Affordable to expensive / 11:30am-6pm Tu-F; to 5 St; from 1pm M

Regent's Park
www.royalparks.gov.uk / 5am-dusk

Orrery, 55 Marylebone High Street, W1U 5 HS / +44 (0)20 77616 8000
www.conran-restaurants.co.uk/restaurants/Orrery
£60 / 12-3pm, 7-11pm; closes 30 min earlier on Sn

The Providores, 109 Marylebone High Street, W1U 4RX
+44 (0)20 7935 6175
www.theprovidores.co.uk / £40
12-2:45pm, 6-10:30pm

Sardo, 45 Grafton Way, W1T 5DQ
+44 (0)20 7387 2521
www.sardo-restauarant.com
£20 / noon-3pm M-F; 6-11pm M-St

Wigmore Hall, 36 Wigmore Street, W1U 2 BP / +44 (0)20 7935 2141
www.wigmore-hall.org.uk / £10-30
Most days at 7:30pm, Monday at 1pm; restaurant opens 2 hours before performances

Dusk, 79 Marylebone High Street, W1U 5JZ / +44 (0)20 7486 5746
10am-11pm M-St; to 10:30pm Sn

Southside Bar, 125 Cleveland St, W1T 6 QB / +44 (0)20 7637 5352
www.southsidebar.co.uk
noon-11pm

Nordic, 25 Newman Street, W1T 1PN / +44 (0)20 7631 3174
www.nordicbar.com
noon-11pm M-F; 6-11pm St

Marquis of Granby, 2 Rathbone Place, W1T 1NT
+44 (0)20 7307 9951 / 11am-11pm

Interval

Halfway Through – Time for the Interval

The London theatre scene has a few quirks, many revolving around the "interval", or intermission. Without doubt the best is the traditional interval treat – ice cream. I'm always sure to carry a few extra pounds in my pocket for this small indulgence.

Another few pounds are stashed away for a programme, which I buy during the intermission (after I've decided whether or not I'd like to remember the show!). The big theatres will usually produce glossy color ones which make great souvenirs.

One of the more obscure interval characters is the "safety curtain", known more archaically as The Iron. My sister and I hypothesized that this was made available to protect the actors from rotten tomatoes, but its actual purpose is a bit less dramatic. In days gone by theatres were lit by gaslight, so a large iron curtain was required by law to seal off the stage area in the event it caught fire. The rule persists, and the safety curtain must be lowered at an appropriate time to prove to the audience that it is in fact functional. These days the safety curtain is usually plain asbestos, but some of the older theatres have beautifully painted ones.

No self-respecting London theatre would be without a bar, which is a great place to join a discussion about the progress of the play over a gin and tonic (G&T). I have often had the luck to eavesdrop on the interval conversations of true theatre aficionados. Keep your ears open and you may have the chance to hear some wonderful stories.

Finally, while Theatreland dominates the scene, I urge fellow theatre lovers to check out a play at any of the many pub theatres scattered throughout London (look in the weekly *Time Out* magazine for details). Some performances compete with the best in London, and the atmosphere is unique. You may even have the chance to buy a pint for the star after the show!

11 Bloomsbury / Clerkenwell

COORDINATES

↑ **15 Islington**
Buses: 19, 38, 341

↑ N

← **2 Mayfair / Soho**
7, 8, 25, 19, 38, 55, 98

Tube Stations: Russell Square
Russell Sq., Tottenham Court Road
A-Z p 61, 62
Farringdon
Holborn, Chancery Lane

→ **12 Shoreditch / Spitalfields**
55, 243

↓ **4 Holborn / Embankment**
17, 45, 46

PROFILE

Special Dates	Day				Night			
	See	Shop	Stroll	Relax	Watch	Eat	Party	Unwind
13x/yr: Designer Warehouse Sales www.designerwarehousesales.com May/Sept: ABCD (Art, Books, Comics, Disney) Show www.bookpalace.com	✓			✓		✓	✓	✓

DOSSIER

Go:	Weekday sightseeing; weeknight unwind
Recognize:	Plunder from Egypt, Greece, Rome
Expect:	Huge crowds at the British Museum; sleepy streets elsewhere
Wear:	Comfortable, mellow, hip casual
Avoid:	Wandering north too close to Euston road
Know:	This is literary London and the ghosts of pens past lazily haunt the area today dominated by the British Museum. Just beyond the museum's shadow are several unique and unusual corners of London with a distinct flavor of daily life. Wandering through Clerkenwell means finding a bar or restaurant that may very well be tomorrow's big thing.

Bloomsbury / Clerkenwell 11

In the morning:

The **British Museum,** the treasure chest of the world, houses the likes of the Rosetta Stone, Elgin Marbles, Sutton Hoo Burial Ship, and numerous Egyptian mummies. It would be easily possible to spend an entire trip in London here and not even scratch the surface, so it is a good idea to investigate the website ahead of time to select a few collections to visit or tours to attend in order to narrow down the field. The museum is often crowded (particularly since admission is free!), so it's worthwhile arriving when it opens at 10 am.

Those who have already visited the British Museum or who want to avoid the crowds should consider visiting the **Foundling Museum**, a 10-minute walk to the east of the BM. This small but moving museum chronicles the history of the first school for orphans and children born to prostitutes during Dickens' day. The top floor is dedicated to school co-founder composer G.F. Handel and is a lovely place to sit and listen to his works.

For lunch:

The British Museum has a restaurant and two cafes, and the Foundling Museum has a pleasant and sunny café with good food. Alternatively, **The Lamb**, nearby at the northern end of Lamb's Conduit, offers an extensive pub menu. Those planning to visit the British Library can dine conveniently at their restaurant or café.

In the afternoon:

The **British Library** is home to mind-boggling masterpieces of the written word. First century Biblical texts, the Magna Carta, original Shakespeare works, ancient copies of the Q'ran and Ramayana are among the breathtaking treasures of their collection. The surrounding area is a nightmare, due more to the massive construction works now taking place rather than former criminal activity, thankfully. The collections are free to visit and rarely swarming with visitors.

11 Bloomsbury / Clerkenwell

Clerkenwell, a hot spot for new bars and renovated pubs, is a gratifying place for an afternoon crawl. Start with the aforementioned Lamb and admire its beautifully preserved bar, original furnishings and cut glass. Continuing down Lamb's Conduit is a lovely old pub, the **Perseverance,** with a nautical theme. There are a handful of pubs along Red Lion Street leading to Holborn High Street, where one of London's most venerable pubs, the **Cittie of Yorke**, is found. From there it's a short walk east to Charterhouse Street, where a number of good spots are located, including funky Japanese kitsch-themed **Fluid**. Heading north on Farringdon Road is **The Eagle**, a classy pub considered one of the pioneers of the "gastropub" trend with a cookbook to its name as a further claim to fame. Gastropubs, which focus on cuisine well beyond the boundaries of traditional pub fare, have blossomed all over London during the last decade and are a uniquely British form of dining.

For dinner:
Konaki, just south of the British Museum, serves top-notch Greek food in a very pleasantly relaxed (and not particularly Greek) atmosphere. Many of the pubs listed on the crawl serve great grub, but the abovementioned Eagle is the star. Lamb's Conduit offers an assortment of delectable restaurants, including Spanish **Cigala** and Italian **Isolabella**, which features live music on Friday and Saturday nights. It's hard to go too far amiss as far as cuisine is concerned in this neighborhood.

In the evening:
When the pub-crawl comes to an end, it's time to hit the dance floor. Clerkenwell boasts two of the best-known dance clubs in London: **Turnmills** and **Fabric**. Both are open late. Dress well, but no need to pull out ostentatious designer threads or outrageous club gear – jeans + cute top = A-OK. They rotate music styles, so be sure to check the website or call ahead to find out what's on.

Bloomsbury / Clerkenwell

Index:
- All times are daily unless noted otherwise, and are subject to change.
- Obtaining a reservation or place on the guest list is always recommended.

British Museum, Great Russell Street, WC1B 3DG
+44 (0)20 7323 8000
www.thebritishmuseum.ac.uk /
£Free 10am-5:30pm; to 8:30pm Th-F; cafes, restaurant open same hours

Foundling Museum, 40 Brunswick Square, WC1N 1AZ
+44 (0)20 7841 3600
www.foundlingmuseum.org.uk / £5
10am-6pm; 12-6pm Sn; closed M

The Lamb, 94 Lamb's Conduit Street, WC1N 3LZ
+44 (0)20 7405 0713
£10 meal / 11am-11pm

British Library, 96 Euston Road, NW1 2DB / +44 (0)870 444 1500
www.bl.uk / £Free / 9:30am-6pm; to 8pm T; to 5pm St; 11am-5pm Sn

Perseverance, 63 Lambs Conduit Street, WC1N 3NB
+44 (0)20 7405 8278 / 11am-11pm

Cittie of Yorke, 22 High Holborn, WC1V 6BN / +44 (0)20 7242 7670
11am-11pm

Fluid, 40 Charterhouse Street, EC1M 6JN / +44 (0)20 7253 3444
www.fluidbar.com / £4 after 10 / bar noon-midnight; DJs 9pm-2am Th-St

The Eagle, 159 Farringdon Road, EC1R 3AL / +44 (0)20 7837 1353
£25 meal / 11am-11pm

Konaki, 5 Coptic Street, WC1A 1NH
+44 (0)20 7580 9730 / £20 / noon-3pm, 5:30-11pm M-F; din only St

Cigala, 54 Lamb's Conduit Street, WC1N 3LW / +44 (0)20 7405 1717
www.cigala.co.uk / £20
noon-10:45pm

Isolabella, 45-46 Red Lion Street, WC1R 4PF / +44 (0)20 7405 6830
£25 / 6-11pm

Turnmills, 63b Clerkenwell Road, EC1M 5NP / +44 (0)20 7250 3409
www.turnmills.co.uk / £10-20
9pm-6am Th-Sn, dates and times vary widely so check the website

Fabric, 77a Charterhouse Street, EC1M 3HN / +44 (0)20 7336 8898
www.fabriclondon.co.uk / £12
10pm-5am F-St

12 Shoreditch / Spitalfields

COORDINATES

↑ <u>15 Islington</u>
Buses: 43, 214, 205, 271

↑N

←
<u>11
Bloomsbury/
Clerkenwell</u>
55, 243

Tube Stations: Old Street

Liverpool Street   A-Z p 64   Shoreditch

Aldgate, Aldgate East

→ <u>N/A</u>

↓ <u>5 City</u>
8, 25, 26, 43, 76, 141, 388

PROFILE

Special Dates	Day				Night			
June/Dec: Spitalfields Festival. Music festival of new and rare works. www.spitalfields festival.org.uk	See	Shop	Stroll	Relax	Watch	Eat	Party	Unwind
	✓	✓					✓	✓

DOSSIER

Go:	Friday and Saturday shopping and partying
Recognize:	Haunts of Jack the Ripper
Expect:	Young, hip, urban Londoners – trendsetters
Wear:	Trendy, sharp casual, comfortable for walking
Avoid:	Wandering north, east or south into Whitechapel, Bethnal Green, Haggerston or De Beauvoir Town – all are still fairly unsavory neighborhoods. Watch your pockets.
Know:	Until recently dingy and derelict, Shoreditch is suddenly seething with cool. This is where the trends are set - from art to clothes to food to clubs. New talent can still afford to move in and have done so in droves. Despite being rough around the edges, east London is rockin'. Get it while it's hot.

Shoreditch / Spitalfields

In the morning:
The **Whitechapel Art Gallery,** a fantastic modern and contemporary art gallery, is a great place to start the day. Located on a grungy street, its exterior is hardly imposing, but the gallery has quietly built its reputation and support. Planned expansion and renovation in 2007 can only mean good things.

For lunch:
The Whitechapel Art Gallery café's lunch options are exceptionally toothsome, even considering the high standards set by London museum fare. Alternatively, try one of several pubs and cafes on Commercial Street outside the Old Spitalfields Market. Avoid the disappointing food sold from stalls within the Market itself.

In the afternoon:
Spitalfields is the perfect place to trend and bargain hunt all afternoon. **Old Spitalfields Market** sells clothes to be unearthed nowhere else. On Sunday it is crowded, noisy, and packed with fierce fashions, many being sold directly by the creative brains behind them. Cutting-edge trends continue at **Frockbrokers, a** short walk from the market, and **Wink**, continuing east.

The area around Brick Lane is better known as the "vintage trail" – stop in at **Rokit** for a treasure quest. Other vintage shops can be more hit and miss but are worth a quick stop for a steal.

Cheshire Street defines boutique heaven. **Beyond Retro** is a vintage emporium. **Labour & Wait** tempts with fun home wares serving double-duty as fantastic souvenirs. **Comfort Station** will doubtless make the accessories junkie feel right at home.

For a further helping of avant-garde take a 20-minute walk north to **The White Cube**, one of London's most prestigious contemporary galleries. The next art movement may be starting there now – pieces on exhibit could very well become the anchors of art collections at the big museums in 40 years' time.

12 Shoreditch / Spitalfields

Spectacularly renovated **Christ Church Spitalfields** is one of the more magnificent of 18th century architect Hawskmoor edifices. Chandeliers, high ceilings, and stained glass make this a sumptuous house of worship.

For dinner:
Hoxton Square has a selection of good restaurants. A favorite is **Cru**, is a front-runner of the Shoreditch scene. Yummy champagne cocktails are their signature beverages.

Nearby Brick Lane has long been renowned as one of the best places in London for dinner – thanks to the prolific and delicious Indian and Bangladeshi food. **Café Naz (and next-door cafeteria)**, right at the south end of the street, has attentive service and Bollywood hits on the big screen, in addition to very tasty fare. Spicy here really means spicy, so order with care!

In the evening:
The triangle formed by Old Street, Curtain Road, and Great Eastern Street, along with Hoxton Square just north, is full of restaurants, bars, clubs, and pubs. It is well worth a wander during daylight hours to get your bearings and then returning after the sun sets. Cool bar **Bluu** has slick drinks and an even better location right on Hoxton Square. For those looking for some bonhomie and a good beer, **Cantaloupe** is one of the several more comfortable pubs and gastropubs in the area. However, the biggest draw to Shoreditch is the number of dance clubs. Be sure to check out the crowds lining up for multi-level, multi-style **333**, '70s disco **Aquarium**, and innovative, superchic **Cargo** to see what takes your fancy.

Whitechapel Art Gallery, 80-82
Whitechapel High Street, E1 7QX
+44 (0)20 7522 7888
www.whitechapel.org / £Free /11am-6pm; to 9pm Th; closed M / café

Old Spitalfields Market
www.visitspitalfields.com

Shoreditch / Spitalfields 12

Frockbrokers, 115 Commercial Street, E1 6BG
+44 (0)20 7247 4222
www.frockbrokers.biz / £Expensive
11am-7pm; to 5:30pm St-Sn

Wink, 20 Hanbury Street, E1 6QR
+44 (0)20 7655 4820 / £Moderate
www.winkclothes.co.uk / 12-7pm

Rokit, 101-107 Brick Lane, E1 6SE
+44 (0)20 77375 3864
www.rokit.co.uk / £Moderate
11am-7pm; 10am-7pm St-Sn

Beyond Retro, 110-112 Cheshire Street, E2 6EJ
+44 (0)20 7613 3636
www.beyondretro.com / £Affordable to expensive / 10am-6pm

Labour & Wait, 18 Cheshire Street, E2 6EH / +44 (0)20 7729 6253
www.labourandwait.co.uk / by appt. Fri; 1-5pm St; 10am-5pm Sn

Comfort Station, 22 Cheshire Street, E2 6EH
+44 (0)20 7033 9099
www.comfortstation.co.uk
£Moderate / 11am-6pm F-Sn

White Cube, 48 Hoxton Square, N1 6PB / +44 (0)20 7930 5373
www.whitecube.com / £Free
10am-6pm; closed Sn, M

Christ Church Spitalfields, Fournier Street, E1 6QE /
+44 (0)20 7859 3035
www.christchurchspitalfields.org / 1-4pm Sn, svc 10:30; 11am-4pm Tu

Cru Restaurant, Bar & Deli, 2-4 Rufus Street, N1 6PE
+44 (0)20 7729 5252
www.cru.co.uk / £35 / noon-3pm; 6-10:30pm; bar open to midnight weekends; closed M

Café Naz, 46-48 Brick Lane, E1 6RF
+44 (0)20 7247 0234
www.cafenaz.co.uk/brick_lane/
£20 / noon to midnight; to 1am Th-St

Bluu, 1 Hoxton Square, N1 6NU
+44 (0)20 7613 2793
www.bluu.co.uk / 11am-11:30pm M-Th; to midnight St; to 10:30 Sn

Cantaloupe Bar & Restaurant, 35 Charlotte Road, EC2A 3PD
+44 (0)20 7613 4411
www.cantaloupe.co.uk / £20
11am-midnight; from noon St

333 Club, 333 Old Street, EC1V 9LE
+44 (0)20 7739 5949
www.333mother.co.uk / £8
10pm-5am

Bar Aquarium, 262-264 Old Street, EC1V 9DD / +44 (0)20 7252 2558
www.clubaquarium.co.uk
£12 / 10pm-5am

Cargo, Kingsland Viaduct, 83 Rivington Street, EC2A 3AY
+44 (0)20 7739 3440
www.cargo-london.com
£10 / 10pm-3am

13 Brixton / Clapham

COORDINATES

↑ *7 Chelsea, 6 Southwark / Lambeth*
Buses: 3, 59 133, 137, 159

↑N

←
Fr. Brixton to Clapham
35, 37, 345

Tube Stations: Clapham North
Clapham Junction *(Rail fr. Waterloo)*
A-Z p 102-104
Brixton
Clapham Common

→
N/A

↓ *N/A*

PROFILE

Special Dates	Day				Night			
	See	Shop	Stroll	Relax	Watch	Eat	Party	Unwind
Jun/Jul: Outdoor concerts www.ticketmaster.co.uk Jul: Sprite Urban Games www.spriteurbangames.com			✓	✓		✓	✓	✓

DOSSIER

Go:	Friday, Saturday daytime chillin'; nighttime party
Recognize:	What it really takes to make life in London a success
Expect:	Brixton: crowds, immigrants, noise, food smells Clapham: Young, cute, white, yuppie families, coffee shops
Wear:	Daytime: very casual, comfortable, neat Nighttime: relaxed club gear, jeans, black boots
Avoid:	Wandering randomly through Brixton, day or night
Know:	Brixton may be outside the comfort zone, but it's as London as Big Ben. London is an immigrant's city – a walk in Brixton Market is like stepping into the West Indies. Clapham, in stark contrast, is much more likely to feel like home away from home, with cute boutiques, quaint coffee shops, and smiling faces.

Brixton / Clapham

In the morning:
For a sensory onslaught go to **Brixton Market**, which resides on Electric Lane and Avenue, spilling into the streets behind the Tube station between Atlantic Road and Coldharbour Lane. Crowded with people who do not look like you, talk like you, act like you, dress like you – it's a whole new side of London. One that smells of incense, butchers, fishmongers, and fruiters. One that sounds of shouts of vendors, blaring music, friends chatting, and some simmering arguments. DO NOT act like a tourist here, especially since you can't help but look like one. Keep your eyes peeled for the high street accessories at a fraction of the price.

For lunch:
On a nice day **Brockwell Park** is a lovely place for lunch. Recently in danger of being razed, in 2001 Lambeth made a commitment to its parks and BP has undergone significant improvements. This true community park boasts a pool (known as "Brixton's Beach"), sport facilities, playgrounds, and an open-air theater for summer concerts. For a picnic, stop at the Costcutter or Super Save on Tulse Hill at the northwest corner of the park.

On a day with less cooperative weather, a trip to the cafes of Clapham High Street or Battersea Rise is in order. **Sea Cow** is good choice for tasty old-fashioned fish 'n chips, and **Lavender**'s mismatched tables and friendly hum are always inviting.

In the afternoon:
Clapham High Street and Battersea Rise flank Clapham Common. The High Street (and The Pavement adjacent) offers a very simple excursion with familiar favorites, like **Body Shop** and **Caffe Nero**, as well as some little gift shops and the like. Battersea Rise, on the other hand, is home to independent restaurants and clothing boutiques. **Mise en Place** is a cheery, comfortable deli and café. And **Katharine Bird** is one of several clothing boutiques worth checking for unique pieces and accessories.

13 Brixton / Clapham

The wide open green space of **Clapham Common** presents a fitting place for stretching the legs on a bright day and watching a pick-up football match. During the summer it also hosts one or more huge outdoor concerts targeted at the under-30 crowd.

For dinner:
Clapham is a marvelous locale to restaurant browse. Battersea Rise, Northcote Road, and Lavender Hill have plenty of eateries. Try **La Pampa** on Battersea Rise for a crowded and friendly Argentine grill; **The Drawing Room**, with its name-matching décor, for an inventive modern menu; or **Bar Meze**, a cheerful and popular Greek place on Northcote Road. Those braving Brixton for dinner need look no further than **Bamboula**. The hut kitsch décor may not be to everyone's taste, but anyone who loves Caribbean fare will find their mouth watering at the generous and tasty plates.

In the evening:
Both Brixton and Clapham boast a busy night scene. Brixton is known for edgy, alternative, rock, indie, and trance – most particularly at the internationally renowned live music venue **Brixton Academy** (which is generally sold out months in advance), but also at famed DJ spot **The Fridge**, a recently refurbished long-time clubbing staple. **Mass** is a popular on-again off-again club in a converted church – it was closed at the time of publishing but is worth checking out.

Clapham is much more clean-cut with out-of-the-box pop. **The Grand,** a recently converted theater, comes complete with a lit dance floor a la Saturday Night Fever, and chart-topping hits till 3 am. Those looking for a more laid-back evening might pursue a pub crawl along Northcote Road.

In the summer, both Brockton Park and Clapham Common host riotous outdoor concerts, which usually include a healthy combination of big names and new talent. Check ticketmaster ahead of time to see if anything's of interest while you're visiting.

Brixton / Clapham

Index:
- All times are daily unless noted otherwise, and are subject to change.
- Obtaining a reservation or place on the guest list is always recommended.

Brixton Market, Electric Avenue, SW9 8JR

Brockwell Park
www.brockwellpark.com

Sea Cow, 57 Clapham High Street, SW4 8NW / +44 (0)20 7622 1537
£12 / noon-11pm Tu-St

The Lavender, 171 Lavender Hill, SW11 5TE / +44 (0)20 7978 5242
£12 / noon-3pm, 7-11pm M-F; 11am-2:30pm, 6:30-11pm St; noon-3 Sn

Caffe Nero www.caffenero.co.uk

Mise en Place, 531 Battersea Rise, SW11 1HH / +44 (0)20 7228 4392
www.thefoodstore.co.uk / £8
8am-8pm M-Sn

Katharine Bird, 20 Battersea Rise, SW11 1EE / +44 (0)20 7228 2235
£Moderate / 10:30am-6pm; to 7 Th; from 10am St; 1-5pm Sn

Clapham Common

La Pampa Grill, 60 Battersea Rise, SW11 1EG / +44 (0)20 7924 4774
£25 / 6pm-midnight

The Drawing Room Restaurant, 103 Lavender Hill, SW11 5QL
+44 (0)20 7350 2564 / £20
noon-11pm

Bar Meze, 54 Northcote Road, SW11 1PA / +44 (0)20 7228 5010
£10 / 6-10pm; to 9:30pm Sn

Bamboula, 12 Acre Lane, SW2 5SG
+44 (0)20 7737 6633 / £10
11am-11pm M-F; noon-11pm St; 3-11pm Sn

Brixton Academy, 211 Stockwell Road SW9 9SL
+44 (0)20 7771 3000
www.brixton-academy.co.uk
£15-50 / days, hours vary

The Fridge, 1 Town Hall Parade, Brixton Hill, SW2 1RJ
+44 (0)20 7326 5100
www.fridgelondon.com / £15
10pm-5am Th-Sn, exact times and dates vary widely, check the website

Mass, St. Matthew's Church, Brixton Hill, SW2 1JF

The Clapham Grand, 21.25 St. John's Hill, SW11 1TT
+44 (0)20 7223 6523
www.leopardclubs.com / £10
10:30pm-3am; to midnight weekdays

14 Hampstead / Camden Town

COORDINATES

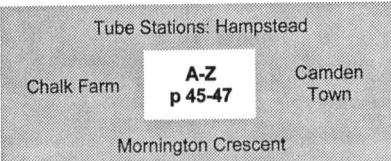

PROFILE

Special Dates	Day				Night			
Summer: Lakeside concerts at Kenwood House. www.picnicconcerts.org	See	Shop	Stroll	Relax	Watch	Eat	Party	Unwind
		✓	✓	✓	✓		✓	

DOSSIER

Go:	Friday and Saturday chillin'; nighttime party
Recognize:	London skyline, your new dream home, birth of punk
Expect:	Hampstead: lovely homes, tree-lined streets, relaxation Camden: noise, crowds, great shopping, bustle, fun
Wear:	Trendy, comfortable casual by day; trendy, edgy by night
Avoid:	Having your pockets picked at the market
Know:	Hampstead High Street is perfect on a sunny Saturday morning; a broad avenue watched over by old oak trees, lined with small shops, cafes, and pubs, and cruised by young families and grandparents. South down the hill into Camden Town brings raucous, bubbling, scurrying activity. The markets boil by day and the music carries on all night.

Hampstead / Camden Town

In the morning:
Two points of interest in Hampstead that will thrill enthusiasts (and likely bore anyone else) are **Fenton House** and **2 Willow Road**. The former, a 17th century mansion with garden, maintains a sublime collection of keyboard instruments from the last four centuries. Permission to play the instruments is granted by audition only, which must be arranged at least one month in advance. Concerts and lectures are held regularly, so check the website before your visit. The latter is the home of the late modern architect Ernö Goldfinger, the design of which is a superior example of the modern movement in Britain, once considered highly controversial for its leftist politics.

Between these two sites is the very beguiling Hampstead High Street, home to several familiar high street shops, and the address of numerous small clothing boutiques and a selection of superb second-hand designer clothes shops.

For lunch:
On Hampstead High Street a branch of London's best chain of cafes, **Giraffe**, serves delicious and nutritious global-themed food in a cheery, communal atmosphere. Those pursuing pub grub on a nice day may prefer the **Freemason's Arms** just outside the heath to sit in their gigantic garden out back. A very classy and quiet gastropub alternative is **Wells**.

In the afternoon:
The crown jewel of Hampstead is **Hampstead Heath**, a semi-wild expanse and a serene place to really stretch your legs, enjoy the fresh air, people-watch, and generally relax. From Downshire Hill, walk past the pond and up the hill through the trees to the crest of **Parliament Hill**, which features a rare panoramic view of London. The heath has swimming ponds, sports grounds, a café, miles of walking paths, and **Kenwood House**, which contains an art gallery and hosts open-air lakeside concerts in the summer.

14 Hampstead / Camden Town

It is a simple bus ride from the square just south of the Hampstead Heath train station into Camden Town, home to the street market pentaverate of **Camden Lock, Camden Canal, Buck Street, Inverness Street,** and **The Stables**. This area once drew London's edgiest, rocking-est crowd, but in recent years developers and yuppies have slowly taken over. That said, there's still no better place to find worn-in Levis, clubbing gear, import furniture, almost-antiques, handmade bongs, and surprises of all kinds – a very amusing place to spend the afternoon. Be prepared for crowds!

For dinner:
Camden is not a particularly inspired place for a meal; however, decent choices include two popular rivals for best Caribbean food in the neighborhood – the **Mango Room** and **Cotton's Rhum Shop, Bar & Restaurant**. An alternative is the **Landsdowne**, a gastropub focusing on tasty organic and free-range produce.

In the evening:
Camden town is packed with bars, pubs, clubs, and performance venues. Check the *Time Out* guide to find out what's happening in the NW1 vicinity. Chalk Farm Road leading onto Camden High Street presents a marvelous setting for a crawl. Noteworthy stops (from north to south) are **Bartok**, London's only classical music DJ bar, **Caernarvon Castle**, a pub with live, loud music, **Electric Ballroom**, pumping oldies but goodies onto their huge dance floor, **Underworld**, a basement showcase of new bands and DJs, and **Koko**, the classily converted Camden Palace theater with a relatively toney crowd.

Hampstead / Camden Town

Fenton House, Windmill Hill, NW3 6RT / +44 (0)20 7435 3471
www.nationaltrust.org.uk ➔ Visits £4.80 / 2-5pm W-F; 11am-5pm St-Sn; closed M, Tu. Hours differ Nov-Mar

2 Willow Road, NW3 1TH
+44 (0)20 7135 6166
www.nationaltrust.org.uk ➔ Visits £4.60 / 12-5pm, Th-St. Hours differ Nov-Mar

Giraffe, 46 Rosslyn Hill, NW3 1NH
+44 (0)20 7 / www.giraffe.net
£10 / 8am-11pm, from 9am on St-Sn

Freemason's Arms, 32 Downshire Hill, NW3 1NT / +44 (0)20 7433 6811 www.freemasonsarms.co.uk / £10 11am-11pm

Wells, 30 Well Walk, NW3 1BX
+44 (0)20 7794 3785
www.thewellshamptead.co.uk
£25 / noon-3pm, 7-10pm M-Th; to 10:30pm F, St; to 9:30pm Sn

Hampstead Heath & Parliament Hill www.cityoflondon.gov.uk ➔ Living Environment ➔ Open Spaces

Kenwood House, Hampstead Lane, NW3 7JR / +44 (0)20 8348 1206
www.english-heritage.co.uk ➔ Properties / £Free / 11am-5pm / café
Concerts: www.picnicconcerts.com

Camden Markets / 10am-6pm
www.camdenlock.net/markets.html

Mango Room, 10-12 Kentish Town Road, NW1 8NX / £20
+44 (0)20 7482 5065 /noon-midnight

Cottons Restaurant, 55 Chalk Farm Road, NW1 8AN
+44 (0)20 7485 8388
www.cottons-restaurant.co.uk
£20 / 6-11pm

Landsdowne, 90 Gloucester Avenue, NW1 8HX
+44 (0)20 7483 0409
£15 / 12-11pm (Sn closed 4-7pm)

Bartok, 78-79 Chalk Farm Road, NW1 8AR / +44 (0)20 7916 0595
5pm-1am; to 2am St; to midnight Sn

Caernarvon Castle, 7-8 Chalk Farm Road, NW1 8AA
+44 (0)20 7284 0219 / noon-1:30pm

Electric Ballroom, 184 Camden High Street, NW1 8QP
+44 (0)20 7485 9006
www.electric-ballroom.co.uk
£10 cover / 10:30am-3:30pm

Underworld, 174 Camden High Street, NW1 0NE
+44 (0)20 7267 3997
www.theunderworldcamden.co.uk
£5-20 cover / 11pm-"late"

Koko, 1a Camden High Street, NW1
+44 (0)870 432 5527 / £7-15 cover
www.koko.co.uk / 10pm-3am F-St

15 Islington

COORDINATES

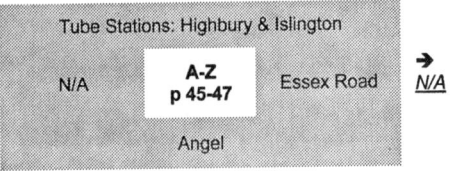

↑N

↑ *N/A*
Buses:

Tube Stations: Highbury & Islington

← *14 Hampstead / Camden* 214, 274

N/A

A-Z p 45-47

Essex Road

→ *N/A*

Angel

↓ *12 Shoreditch / Spitalfields* 43, 214, 205, 271

PROFILE

Special Dates	Day				Night			
	See	Shop	Stroll	Relax	Watch	Eat	Party	Unwind
Jan: London Art Fair. All UK galleries and dealers under one roof. www.londonartfair.co.uk		✓	✓	✓	✓	✓	✓	✓

DOSSIER

Go:	Friday, Saturday chillin', nighttime party
Recognize:	If you're Bethany, everything! Welcome home.
Expect:	Young, hip, single crowd
Wear:	Trendy casual, comfortable for walking
Avoid:	Wandering too far down Essex Road into the projects or north on Holloway Road
Know:	Islington was one of the first neighborhoods to benefit from the economic boom in London over the last decade. Once a rundown hangout for hoodlums, today it's a fun, vibrant, diverse neighborhood, bursting with character and an easy place to call home. It's an aspiring performer's dream, with a theater around practically every corner.

Islington 15

In the morning:
The **Euphorium** bakery is a perfect stop for a morning treat and a cup of coffee right at the top of the shopping district extending over a mile south down Upper Street.

Modern art cognoscente (and those who aspire to such) will want to visit the quirky **Estorick Collection**, a small gallery devoted primarily to Italian Futurist art and Fascist propaganda centered on flight technology in the '30s.

For lunch:
The Estorick has a little café in a pleasant courtyard. Just around the corner is the **Canonbury**, a pub with a really tempting menu and a great beer garden out back. At the south end of Islington on Essex Road is a branch of **Giraffe**, London's best chain of cafes with a world food and music focus.

In the afternoon:
Islington offers remarkable and affordable shopping all along Upper Street and neighboring Cross Street. At the south end by the intersection (and Tube station) known as "Angel" find the new N1 outdoor mall, home to high street favorites **Accessorize**, **Oasis** and **French Connection**. Farther north are independent shops such as trendy **Diverse** and sexy lingerie boutique **Tallulah**, among many others. Bargain hunters should stop in **Seconda Mano** to check out the lightly used designer threads. Islington also features a fab assortment of gift shops and home wares shops, so this is a wonderful choice to shop for souvenirs for self and friends back home. The **Camden Passage Antiques Market** must not be overlooked – in quality it easily rivals Portobello Road.

Rainy afternoons can be brightened with a trip to Islington's friendly little single-screen theater, **The Screen on the Green**, which always features funky foreign flicks along with the blockbusters. For more unique entertainment, check to see if the **Little Angel** puppet theater plans to put on a show and hang out with the kids.

15 Islington

However, an afternoon in Islington may be best spent on a pub crawl. It's easiest to begin north (at the *top* of the big hill) with a visit to the **Canonbury**. From there it's a quick skip to classy but relaxed neighborhood hangout **25 Canonbury Lane**. Around the corner is **the garden**, with outdoor seating on the street and an extensive list of beers on tap. From here there are no less than 30 pubs and bars on Upper Street and nearby Essex Road and Liverpool Road. The closer to Angel, the more likely to run into chain bars such as the relatively refined Slug & Lettuce and Pitcher & Piano, and wild Walkabout and O'Neill's.

For dinner:
Choose from many dining options in Islington. Favorites include the atmospheric and delicious **Montmartre** to the south on Essex Road, and friendly, casually romantic **Cantina Italia** at the north end on Canonbury Lane. In between the two is **Pasha**, boasting superb Turkish fare. Those attending a performance at the Almeida or the King's Head may want to dine at their respective restaurants.

In the evening:
Islington is the best place outside of Theatreland to catch a performance on the boards. Top-tier **Almeida,** accustomed to rave reviews and sold-out performances, keeps attracting better and more famous talent (note 2005's appearance by sizzling Gael Garcia Bernal). Just south of Angel is **Sadler's Wells**, London's premier dance hall and frequent exhibitor of top international talent. Upper Street is home to no less than three pub theaters: **The King's Head,** the most well-known, puts on ambitious renditions of popular plays. It sits right in the center of Upper Street, which is book-ended by the **Hen & Chicks** to the north and the **Old Red Lion** to the south, both specializing in first or second productions of edgy contemporary drama.

Islington may be even better known for entertainment of a sweatier kind, as the residence of **Arsenal F.C.**, a world-class football team.

Tickets to a home game must be booked as far in advance as possible. Remember that football *is* life in Britain, so acting like an idiot at a match is likely to result in injury. Behave.

Late-night around Angel is a lively yet more relaxed place to party than many other parts of town. Consider **Embassy**, a hip DJ bar, **Elbow Room**, with R&B dance beats and American-style pool tables, and funky **Clockwork**, with unusual music and even more unusually flavored vodkas (like Marmite!).

Index:
- All times are daily unless noted otherwise, and are subject to change.
- Obtaining a reservation or place on the guest list is always recommended.

Euphorium Bakery, 202 Upper Street, N1 1RQ
+44 (0)20 7704 6905 / £4
7am-11pm M-Th; to midnight F-St; from 9am Sn

Estorick Collection, 39a Canonbury Square, N1 2AN
+44 (0)20 7704 9522
www.estorickcollection.com / £3.50
11am-6pm W-St; 12-5pm Sn; closed M, Tu

Canonbury, 21 Canonbury Place, N1 2NS / +44 (0)20 7288 9881
noon-11pm

Giraffe, 29-31 Essex Road, N1 2SA
+44 (0)20 7359 5999
www.giraffe.net / £10
8am-11pm; from 9am St-Sn

Accessorize
www.accessorize.co.uk

Oasis www.oasis-stores.com

FCUK (French Connection)
www.fcuk.com

Diverse, 294 Upper Street, N1 2TU
+44 (0)20 7359 8877 / £Moderate
10:30am-6pm; to 7:30 Th; 12:30-6pm Sn

Tallulah, 65 Cross Street, N1 2BB
+44 (0)20 7704 0066 / £Moderate
11am-6:30pm M-St; noon-4pm Sn

Seconda Mano, 111 Upper Street, N1 1QN / +44 (0)20 7359 5284 / £Affordable-Expensive / 10am-5pm M-T; to 8pm W, F, St; 11am-5pm Sn

Camden Passage Antiques Market, N1 8EG
+44 (0)20 7359 0190
www.camdenpassageantiques.com
£Varies / Arcade open W, St; shops open 7 days

15 Islington

Screen on the Green, 83 Upper Street, N1 0NP
+44 (0)20 7226 3520
www.screencinemas.co.uk
£4.80 M, and before 5:30pm; £7

Little Angel Theatre, 41 Dagmar Passage, N1 2DN
+44 (0)20 7226 1787
www.littleangeltheatre.com / £7.50
times vary, check in advance

25 Canonbury Lane, N1 2AS
+44 (0)20 7226 0955/ £10
5pm-11:30pm; from 1pm St-Sn

the garden, 179 Upper Street, N1 1RG / +44 (0)20 7226 6276
noon-11pm M-W; to midnight Th; to 2am F-St; to 10:30pm Sn

Montmartre, 196 Essex Road, N1 8LZ / +44 (0)20 7688 1497 / £15
10am-11pm

Cantina Italia, 19 Canonbury Lane, N1 2AS / +44 (0)20 7226 9791
£15 / 6:30pm-11pm; also noon-3pm St-Sn

Almeida Theatre, Almeida Street, N1 1TA / =+44 (0)20 7359 5404
www.almeida.co.uk / £5-50
M-St 7:30pm; Sn 3:30pm

Sadler's Wells, Roseberry Avenue, EC1R 4TN / +44 (0)870 737 7737
www.sadlerswells.com / £15-50
times vary

The King's Head, 115 Upper Street N1 1QN / +44 (0)20 7226 1916
www.kingsheadtheatre.org / £10-20
8pm Tu-St; 3:30pm St-Sn

Hen & Chickens Theatre, 109 St. Pauls Road, N1 2NA
+44 (0)20 7704 2001
www.henandchickens.com
£10 tix, cash only / pub noon-11pm; show 8pm Tu-St, 5pm Sn

Old Red Lion Theatre, 418 St John Street, EC1V 4NJ
+44 (0)20 7837 7816
www.oldredliontheatre.com
£8-20 tix / times vary

Arsenal F.C., Avenell Road, N5 1BU
+44 (0)20 7704 4040
www.arsenal.com / £28-50 / times vary. Box O. open 9:30am-5pm M-F

Embassy Bar, 119 Essex Road, N1 2SN / +44 (0)20 7226 7901
www.embassybar.com / 11am-midnight, to 2am weekends

Elbow Room, 89-91 Chapel Market
+44 (0)20 7278 3244
www.theelbowroom.co.uk / noon-2am; to 3am F-St; to midnight Sn-M

Clockwork, 96-98 Pentonville Road, N1 9JB / +44 (0) 7837 5387 / £5-15
noon-11pm; to 3am weekends

Greenwich 16

COORDINATES

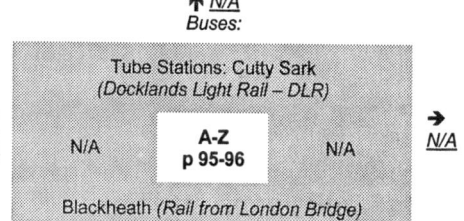

↑ *N/A*
Buses:

↑**N**

Tube Stations: Cutty Sark
(Docklands Light Rail – DLR)

← *London* 188 or Ferry | N/A | **A-Z p 95-96** | N/A | → *N/A*

Blackheath *(Rail from London Bridge)*

↓ *N/A*

PROFILE

Special Dates	Day				Night			
April: London Marathon www.london-marathon.co.uk Jul: Greenwich & Docklands Intl. Festival www.festival.org	See	Shop	Stroll	Relax	Watch	Eat	Party	Unwind
	✓		✓	✓				✓

DOSSIER

Go:	Weekday sightsee and stroll
Recognize:	Canary Wharf and Thames Flood Barrier
Expect:	Laid back town, some tourists at key sights
Wear:	Casual, comfortable for walking
Avoid:	
Know:	Greenwich is an historic and beautiful maritime village tucked away on the western reaches of the Thames, just south of the skyscrapers of Canary Wharf. It's the starting place for the London Marathon and the standard by which we set our clocks, former home to royalty and current home to families looking for a little peace and quiet. It's a link with seafaring history and a lovely place to just relax.

16 Greenwich

In the morning:
There are two picturesque approaches to the key sights of Greenwich. For a leisurely view of London, pick up the ferry at Westminster Pier. Service begins at 10 am and ferries leave every 40 minutes. The ride runs approximately an hour. Alternatively, take national rail from London Bridge to Blackheath station and saunter across the heath to Greenwich Park.

Within Greenwich Park are several sights worth visiting. Perhaps most famous is the **Prime Meridian Line**, dividing the east and west hemispheres. Just behind it is the **Old Royal Observatory**, which describes the fascinating search to find the method to measure longitude at sea. Greenwich Mean Time is officially clocked and displayed here. At the bottom of the hill is the **National Maritime Museum**, chronicling Britain's vastly impressive naval history.

Docked on the river is the **Cutty Sark**, the 1869 tea clipper that broke the world record from London to China, a critical component in the tea trade. Climb aboard and step back in time to the days of the Empire.

If you have already visited these top Greenwich sites consider taking in the art collection of the **Rangers House** in the south end of Greenwich Park or the painting collection in the **Old Royal Naval College**.

For lunch:
On a nice day a picnic in the park is quite pleasant – consider bringing along a Frisbee or cricket bat and while away the afternoon. A quick trip to the Co-op grocery store on Trafalgar Road will provide outdoor dining provender. If the weather's not conducive, consider the scores of pubs down by the Cutty Sark, such as the **Gipsy Moth**, for some bangers 'n mash, or the Regatta Café or Upper Deck Coffee Bar at the National Maritime Museum.

Greenwich 16

In the afternoon:

It's possible to spend the entire afternoon taking in the sights that didn't fit in before lunch and strolling through the Park. Also in order is a visit to the low-key **Greenwich Market**, which focuses on antiques on Thursdays, farmers' produce on Fridays, and arts and crafts from Thursday through Sunday.

For those seeking something tranquilly different, visit the unusual **Fan Museum** and include their lovely afternoon tea, served after 3 pm on Tuesdays and Saturdays in the Orangery.

Engineering votaries may prefer to proceed slightly farther west to the **Thames Flood Barrier**. As few as 50 years ago hundreds of people died when the tidal Thames broke its banks. Huge hydraulic gates were installed in the '70s to control its ebb and flow. Call in advance to find out when they will be tested or in operation for an awesome display.

For dinner:

A neighborhood favorite is **Inside**, which has a varied and tasty menu and casual, welcoming atmosphere. A pub with a little of everything, including a fire in winter and lovely garden in the summer, is the **Ashburnham Arms**, which also does a respectable pub menu.

Greenwich is a long way from home base, so you may instead want to start heading back in towards town. A truly memorable stop for a seafood meal and a couple of pints is **The Grapes**, a fantastic old pub in Limehouse on the north bank. Take the DLR (Docklands Light Rail) from the Cutty Sark to Westferry. A bonus – the DLR travels right through the center of Canary Wharf for an inspiring view of all the new skyscrapers.

16 Greenwich

Index:
- All times are daily unless noted otherwise, and are subject to change.
- Obtaining a reservation or place on the guest list is always recommended.

National Maritime Museum, including Old Royal Observatory, Greenwich, SE10 9NF
+44 (0)20 8312 6565
www.nmm.ac.uk / £Free / 10am-5pm

Cutty Sark, King William Walk, Greenwich, SE10 9HT
+44 (0)20 8858 3445
www.cuttysark.org.uk / £4.50
10am-5pm

Ranger's House, Chesterfield Walk, Blackheath, SE10 8QX
+44 (0)20 8853 0035
www.english-heritage.org.uk → Properties / £5.30
10am-5pm W-Sn Mar-Sep. Other months by appt. only.

Old Royal Naval College, 2 Cutty Sark Gardens, Greenwich SE10 9LW / +44 (0)20 8269 4747
www.greenwichfoundation.org.uk
£Free / 10am-5pm

Gipsy Moth, 60 Greenwich Church Street, Greenwich, SE10 9BL
+44 (0)20 8858 0786 / £10
noon-11pm; to 10:30pm Sn

Greenwich Market
www.greenwichmarket.co.uk

Fan Museum, 12 Crooms Hill, Greenwich, SE10 8ER
+44 (0)20 8305 1441
www.fan-museum.org / £3.50
11am-5pm; noon-5pm Sn; closed M

Thames Flood Barrier
www.environment-agency.gov.uk/regions/thames/ → Key Issues → Flooding → Thames Barrier

Inside, 19 Greenwich South Street, SE10 8NW / +44 (0)20 8265 5060
www.insiderestaurant.co.uk / £15
6:30-11pm Tu-St; noon-2:30pm W-Sn

Ashburnham Arms, 25 Ashburnham Grove, SE10 8UH
+44 (0)20 8692 2007 / £12
noon-11pm M-St; to 10:30pm Sn

The Grapes, 76 Narrow Street, E14 8BP / +44 (0)20 7987 4396 / £10
noon-11pm

Farther Afield

A handful of points outside of central London, but still on the Tube, don't require a full day trip to visit and are worth the couple of extra pounds to roam outside Zone 2.

(north past Hampstead-14) **Highgate Cemetery**

The list of London notables buried here is extensive and the grounds are, ahem, hauntingly beautiful. Tours of the special Eastern Cemetery, which occur weekdays at 2 pm and at several times on weekends, must be booked in advance, a worthwhile effort for those planning on making the journey up to Highgate. The Western Cemetery is open to all during daylight hours.

Swains Lane, N6 6JP / +44 (0)20 8340 1834 / http://highgate-cemetery.org
£3 / tour 2pm weekdays, on the hour from 11am-4pm weekends

(southwest past Chelsea-7) **Kew Gardens**

The highlight of this large and lovely park is the beautifully restored Victorian greenhouse, home to plants from all over the former empire. The many other conservatories and exhibits show rare and wonderful flora from around the world. The Gardens has an appealing café, or for a picnic stop at the small grocery store outside of the station.

Royal Botanic Gardens, Kew, Richmond, Surrey, TW9 3AB
+44 (0)20 8332 5655 / www.rbgkew.org.uk / £10
9:30am-5pm; to 6pm during summer

(southwest past Chelsea-7) **Richmond Park**

Richmond itself is a very charming little town – an inviting place for a walk and a cup of tea. The Great Park is a huge expanse, partially wooded and still home to many red deer. If the London heat feels oppressive, this is *the* place to escape for the afternoon.

Richmond Park Office, Holly Lodge, Bog Lodge Yard, Richmond Park, Surrey. TW10 5HS / +44 (0)20 8948 3209 / www.royalparks.gov.uk
7:30am-dusk

Even Farther Afield – Day Trips

Visitors who have a day to spare should consider these scenic day trips, each less than 90 minutes from London. Train timetables are available at www.nationalrail.co.uk. Travels who want somebody else to mind the details should check www.walks.com.

Bath
Visit the Roman Baths that gave this charming riverside hamlet its name. Walk the neighborhoods of lovely homes and follow the footsteps of Virginia Woolfe.   Paddington Station / www.visitbath.co.uk

Cambridge
Wander the hallowed halls of learning. Stroll the willowed paths and take a punt on the Cam.   King's Cross Station / www.visitcambridge.org

Canterbury
Haunt the streets with the ghosts of Chaucer's Tales, then renew your awe at the Cathedral.   Victoria Station / www.visitcanterbury.co.uk

Hampton Court Palace
Revisit Henry VIII in this most incredible of England's castles, then get lost in the hedge maze.   Waterloo Station / www.hrp.org.uk

Leeds Castle
Not called "the loveliest castle in the world" in vain! This lakeside stronghold is truly picturesque.   Victoria Station / www.leeds-castle.com

Oxford
From the cobbled streets to the dreamy spires, Oxford is everything it's cracked up to be. Raise a pint to Tolkein, Lewis, and friends at the Eagle and Child.   Paddington Station / www.oxford.gov.uk/tourism/

Windsor Castle
You probably won't be able to take tea with the Queen, but the Castle is fascinating nevertheless. Take a long walk through the great park with an eye peeled for deer.
                              Waterloo Station / www.windsor.gov.uk

Weekend Getaways – Farthest Afield

Visitors making an extended stay in London may wish to get away from the hustle and bustle for a couple of days. Serene and romantic options include:

Cornwall
Palm trees, dolphins, fishing villages, and savory pasties (hearty regional pies) make this one of the more unusual and charming corners of England. World-famous Stonehenge is along the way.
Paddington Station / www.cornwalltouristboard.co.uk

Edinburgh
It's impossible to describe the goose bump-inducing power of the towers and fells of this city, which is nevertheless amiable and extremely accessible. Good luck figuring out what the locals are saying, but the only regret a visitor to Edinburgh has is the advent of their departure date.   King's Cross Station / www.edinburgh.gov.uk

Lakes District
The Lakes District is renowned for its beauty. It's crowded during the summer but makes a superb getaway any time of year. Be sure to visit Beatrix Potter's house, which by her request has been left as if she just popped down to the shop and is expected back at any moment.   Euston Station / www.cumbria-the-lakes-district.co.uk

Norfolk Broads
A favorite Easter holiday weekend pastime is boating the Norfolk Broads. These canals were dredged for peat and then used to transport it, but now they make a highly pleasant route for the specially-designed broadboats, which are child's play to maneuver.
Liverpool Street Station / www.broads-authority.gov.uk

Paris
What's better than a stroll along the Seine? Thanks to Eurostar, it's a snap to journey straight from central London to central Paris with zero airport-style hassle.   Waterloo Station / www.eurostar.com

Resources

Before You Go

Plan Your Trip	88
Book This Now	91
Accommodation	92
Specialty Guides	96

When You Arrive

Get Oriented	97
Get Around	98
Get Connected	100

While You're There

Make Friends	102
Down the Pub	107
Speak Well	110
Save Money	113
Discover Secret London	117
Emergency Information / Personal Safety	119

Index

120

Plan Your Trip

When to go
The best months are April and October, with plenty of daylight, decent weather, lower prices, and light tourist volume. September and May have better weather, higher prices, and relatively few tourists. Summer months are hot, humid, expensive, and crowded. Winter months can be very cold, but prices are low, there is little competition for accommodation, and often no queues at the sights.

Note that almost everything is closed on Bank Holidays: 1/1, Good F, Easter M, first & last M in May, last M in Aug, 12/25-12/26.

Papers in order
Visitors must possess a passport valid for at least six months from the date of entry into the country. Note that it takes six weeks to process a first-time application for a passport. More information can be found at http://travel.state.gov/passport.

US citizens can stay in the UK for up to six months without a visa, as long as they have the funds to support their stay without working. To stay longer, a visa is required. More information is available at www.ukvisas.gov.uk.

US citizens are not eligible for health care coverage in the UK, so visitors must purchase medical insurance in the US prior to the trip (if not already covered under their existing insurance policy).

Do not neglect to make a photocopy of your passport, any visas, health insurance policy, tickets, and any other vital documents. Keep the copies separate from the originals in case of loss or theft.

Buying plane tickets
It is well worth shopping around for plane tickets. During the off season, round-trip non-stop direct flights from many major cities can be as low as $350 including taxes and fees, so check in regularly at travel and airline websites. Expect to pay double during the summer.

Plan Your Trip

Staying Healthy

Nothing ruins a trip like catching a cold or the flu on the flight over, but it's a risk because of extended exposure on the plane and the fact that most people need to work long hours before a trip. Be sure to wash your hands frequently on the plane and don't touch your face. During the two weeks leading up to your trip, be sure to:

- Get plenty of sleep.
- Eat a balanced diet.
- Take a daily multi-vitamin.
- Take a daily immune system booster, e.g. Airborne.
- Drink lots of water.
- Get in 45 minutes of walking per day.

Daily itineraries

It's impossible to see everything in London and a visit will certainly be ruined by frantic sightseeing. To keep the trip enjoyable:

- **Pick one priority each day.** A good rule of thumb is to ask each person in the party to write down two or three personal "must-sees" for the trip and assign a day to each one. That way nobody leaves London without having seen or done what was most important to them.

- **Leave some chill-out time.** If, for example, the morning is spent at the Tate Modern, schedule time in the afternoon to walk along the river and sit down for a pint or two. There's only so much structured culture one can soak up in a day, so preserve time in each day to just be.

- **Have "free" days.** It's nice to have even just one day where you don't have to feel guilty about sleeping in and watching TV. It's also likely that once in London you'll discover more things to do, and favorite activities or sites you'll hope to repeat or revisit. Leave time for those occasions in your schedule.

Plan Your Trip

- **Visit one neighborhood at a time**. Public transportation in London is remarkable, but it can be stressful and time-consuming. Don't spend more time commuting than you need to.
- **Practice saying "next time."** Remember, a sight or pub missed is not one lost – rather, it's an ideal reason to return to London that much sooner.

What to pack

London is a fashion capital of the world, so a trip to London is a good excuse to be your best-dressed every day. Combined with the variable weather, this makes over-packing a real risk on a London trip. Pick a single color scheme so that tops, bottoms, shoes, bags, coats, jackets, and accessories are as interchangeable as possible.

Weather information is available at: www.bbc.co.uk/weather and www.weather.com. Assume it's going to pour at least one day on your trip. This can be a good excuse to buy a hip new raincoat (which doubles as a great souvenir).

Special things to keep in mind are:

- **Power converters** – the power system is different, so purchase a converter for any electronic devices.
- **Money** – only a small amount of petty cash is necessary to pack, as ATMs accept most cash cards throughout London. Current exchange rates are available online at financial sites like http://finance.yahoo.com/currency.
- **Papers** – bring a photocopy of vital documents, such as passport, visa, tickets, and insurance place.

One final packing note: With the millions of pieces of baggage going through Gatwick and Heathrow airports, you'll be more likely to be reunited with your own if your luggage isn't black like everyone else's!

Book This Now

For a prayer of guaranteeing a time or a ticket, check or book the following as far in advance as possible:

Sports
- Arsenal F.C. (Islington) www.arsenal.com
- Chelsea F.C. (Chelsea) www.chelseafc.com
- Lords Cricket Ground (Marylebone) www.lords.org

Entertainment
- Brixton Academy Concerts (Brixton) www.brixton-academy.co.uk
- Brockwell Park Concerts (Brixton) www.ticketmaster.co.uk/venue/279237
- Clapham Common Concerts www.ticketmaster.co.uk/venue/198209
- Globe Theatre (Southwark) www.shakespeares-globe.org
- Other Pop Concerts (All) www.ticketmaster.co.uk
- Other Theatre (Theatreland, Islington) www.officiallondontheatre.co.uk
- Royal Albert Hall (Knightsbridge) www.royalalberthall.com
- Royal Festival Hall (Southwark) www.rfh.org.uk
- Royal Opera & Ballet (Covent Garden) www.royalopera.org
- Wigmore Hall (Marylebone) www.wigmore-hall.org.uk

Events
- A&D Gallery Soirees (Marylebone) www.a-and-d.co.uk
- Chelsea Flower Show (Chelsea) www.rhs.org.uk
- London Fashion Week (Chelsea) www.londonfashionweek.co.uk
- Thames Barrier (Greenwich) www.environment-agency.gov.uk/regions/thames/ → Key Issues → Flooding → Thames Barrier

Sights
- Fenton House Auditions (Hampstead) www.nationaltrust.org.uk → Visits → Fenton House
- Highgate Cemetery (Afield) http://highgate-cemetery.org
- Lambeth Palace (Lambeth) www.lambethpalacelibrary.org
- Swiss Re Building, a.k.a. "The Gherkin" (City) www.30stmaryaxe.com

Restaurants
- The Ivy (Soho) www.caprice-holdings.co.uk

Accommodation

The neighborhood in London with the optimal combination of location, transportation access, amenities, and price is boring but convenient **Bayswater**, just north of Hyde Park and Kensington Gardens, and south and west of Paddington Station (where the Heathrow Express terminates). Its thoroughfare Queensway (and, to a lesser extent, Craven Road) has grocery stores, newsagents, chemists (pharmacies), mobile phone retailers, internet cafes, plenty of pubs, and even rarities like an ice rink, bowling alley, and a shopping mall with a cinema. Restaurants in the area range from crap to passable.

COORDINATES

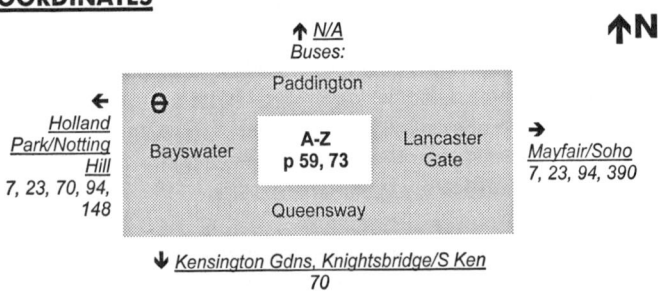

All prices are for a double *en suite* (with a bathroom) including breakfast and VAT (Value Added Tax). All accept credit cards unless otherwise stated.

Craven Gardens Hotel, 16 Leinster Terrace, W2 3EU
www.cravengardenshotel.com / +44 (0)20 7262 3167
£65 / 43 rooms (all non-smoking) / Students in the bar, big breakfast buffet

Barry House Hotel, 12 Sussex Place, W2 2TP
www.barryhouse.co.uk / +44 (0)20 7723 7340
£73 / 18 rooms (3 n.s.) / Smart and family-run

Accommodation

Byron Hotel, 36-38 Queensborough Terrace, W2 3SH
+44 (0)20 7243 0987
£75 / 45 rooms (all n.s.) / Well-restored, modern facilities

Kingsway Park Hotel, 139 Sussex Gardens, W2 2RX
www.kingswaypark-hotel.com / +44 (0)20 7723 5677
£76 / 22 rooms (8 n.s.) / Modern art in public areas

Park Lodge Hotel, 73 Queensborough Terrace, W2 3SU
+44 (0)20 7229 6424
£85 / 29 rooms (all n.s.) / Restored former townhouse; power showers

Delmere, 130 Sussex Gardens, W2 1UB
www.delmerehotels.com / +44 (0)20 7706 3344
£96 / 35 rooms (10 n.s.) / Friendly, warm; bar and lounge

Blakemore Hotel, 30 Leinster Gardens, W2 3AN
www.starcrown.com / +44 (0)20 7262 4591
£116 / 164 rooms (28 n.s.) / Quiet, neat; restaurant and bar

Norfolk Plaza Hotel, 29-33 Norfolk Square, W2 1RX
www.norfolkplazahotel.co.uk / +44 (0)20 7723 0792
£136 / 87 rooms (58 n.s.) / Popular, friendly; bar and lounge

Mornington Hotel, 12 Lancaster Gate, W2 3LG
www.bw-morningtonhotel.co.uk / +44 (0)20 7762 7361
£140 / 66 rooms (27 n.s.) / Fine Victorian building, modern bedrooms; big Scandinavian breakfast

Gresham Hyde Park, 66 Lancaster Gate, W2 3NZ
www.gresham-hotels.com / +44 (0)20 7262 5090
£195 / 188 rooms (77 n.s.) / Landmark building, genteel; modern bedrooms and exercise facilities

Accommodation

Evaluating other options:
Key considerations when evaluating candidates are:

- **Location**. Type the postcode (e.g. W2 3NZ) into www.streetmap.co.uk. If there are not at least two Zone 1 or Zone 2 Tube stops (on different lines) within adjacent map squares, it is too far out and too poorly connected. (Tube map available on www.tfl.gov.uk.)

- **Noise**. Again, enter the postcode into streetmap. If the hotel is on a street colored yellow, pink, or green, it is going to be busy and loud. Call to in advance to discuss noise levels and obtain a room facing away from the street.

- **Plumbing**. Call and confirm shower pressure in advance. Many buildings have old plumbing and poor water pressure.

- **Air conditioning**. London can be uncomfortably hot and humid in the late spring and throughout the summer. Call ahead to discuss ventilation. Those sensitive to the heat should find accommodation with air conditioning in July and August.

- **Bathrooms**. Be sure to confirm that the room is "en suite" – has its own bathroom. Many bed & breakfasts have a common bathroom per floor rather separate bathrooms per room.

Cost-effective accommodation:
Accommodation can easily become the largest expense, so it's worthwhile thoroughly investigating the options, particularly if you are planning on staying more than a couple of days.

- **B&Bs** – Two reputable organizations that focus solely on evaluating bed & breakfasts and making placements within London are www.bulldogclub.com and www.lhslondon.co.uk.

- **House swap** – Those planning on an extended stay with some flexibility may want to seek a home swap partner. Start looking at http://london.craigslist.com.

Accommodation

Recommendations from friends:

Specialty Guides

London Moxie is intentionally concise to make it easy to tote in a bag or a pocket. For more details, here are the authoritative resources on everything that doesn't fit within these pages.

- **See** *Blue Guide Museums and Galleries of London* is updated regularly and provides reviews on museum restaurants, too. *Discovering London Statues and Monuments* covers the host of memorialized notables. *A Guide to the Architecture of London* is about a decade out of date but is otherwise excellent.
- **Shop** *Time Out London Shopping* is revamped each year and is the definitive London shopping guide. Popular *London Markets* by Cadogan Guides is releasing its 4th edition in 2006.
- **Stroll** *Time Out London Walks* has multiple volumes and editions of illustrated walks by London artists and celebrities.
- **Relax** *London Gardens: A Seasonal Guide* covers green spaces large and small. *The Ritz Guide to Afternoon Tea* is a charming etiquette lesson as well as cookbook.
- **Watch** Anyone unfamiliar with the insane popularity of soccer must get *The Complete Encyclopedia of Football*. Theatre buffs will want their own copy of *The Great Theatres of London*.
- **Eat** *Time Out Eating & Drinking* is the annual London restaurant Bible. *Time Out Cheap Eats in London* keeps budgets on track.
- **Party** *Time Out Bars, Pubs, & Clubs* goes from cozy to swanky and will no doubt help you get your drink on.
- **Unwind** Not surprisingly, there are a number of websites in London dedicated just to pubs. Check out www.fluidfoundation.com.
- **Accommodation** Fodor's is the champ at uncovering gems for any budget.
- **History** *The Times History of London* gives a thorough but very manageable overview in 192 pages.

Get Oriented

London is one of the most confusing cities on the planet to navigate, due to the absence of a grid pattern street layout, clearly posted street signs, consistent building numbering, or dependably visible landmarks. The following resources are critical to achieving independence in London:

Spiral-Bound London mini A-Z
The *London A-Z* is a <u>complete</u> indexed street map of London. All Londoners own one. The spiral-bound mini version (referenced in this book) is handy for visitors because it fits in a bag and stays open easily. Pick one up today at www.a-zmaps.co.uk

www.streetmap.co.uk
This online London street map can look up any address or postcode and display a printable map of the area. www.streetmap.co.uk

The Original London Walks
This company provides superior walking tours of nearly every neighborhood in London, giving great on-the-ground orientation. Don't fall for imitators – these guys are the best. www.walks.com

Bus Tours
There are several bus tour companies that make the rounds of central London, which can be a good introduction to the lay of the land on your first day. www.theorginaltour.com, www.bigbus.co.uk

Take the Bus
The London bus system is overwhelming as a whole, and slow for traveling across town when compared to the Tube. But for traveling to an adjacent neighborhood it is easy and fast, and can really help to "connect the dots" between neighborhoods. The bus system has undergone massive renovations over the last couple of years. The nostalgic old double-deckers are gone, but instead most stops have a reader-board advising travelers of the arrival time of the next buses, and CCTV keeps all routes safe and sound. www.tfl.gov.uk

Get Around

All of London's public transportation information is on a single website – Transport for London, www.tfl.gov.uk. Some brief tips:

Cars
Cars are worse than useless in London. Do not rent one.

The Zones
The London transportation system is set up in roughly concentric circles called Zones, with Zone 1 being the innermost. Zones 1 and 2 comprise central London, including all neighborhoods covered in this guidebook. Visitors rarely have occasion to exit Zone 2.

Travel Passes
A 3-Day Zones 1 and 2 Travel Pass offers significant savings (as much as 50 percent or more). It can be purchased for £15 at any Tube station in Zones 1 and 2 and is accepted on the Tube, buses, and in-city rail.

The Tube (London Underground)
This is usually the fastest way across town, but not necessarily any faster or easier between adjacent neighborhoods, when it is usually more convenient to take the bus. Be aware that the Tube stops running between 11:30 and midnight, so if you plan on staying out late check the night bus schedule in advance (or be prepared to take a cab). The Tube map is available to download online. Note that "subway" in London refers to a pedestrian underpass.

Buses
Taking a bus across town is time-consuming, but riding the bus between adjacent neighborhoods is often the quicker, easier, and more pleasant option when compared to the Tube. After 11:30-ish the Night Buses (which are slightly different than the day routes) are the only form of public transportation in London – be forewarned that cabs can be hard to find. Bus maps (including the much more useful new "Spider" maps) are available to download from the website.

Get Around

Black Cabs

This is the quintessential London form of transport. All Black Cab drivers really do have "The Knowledge" – it takes years for the cabbies to learn every last London street and alleyway. Black Cabs are always professional– they're also expensive, and when the traffic is bad not necessarily any faster than public transportation.

Note that there are other cab companies in London, some of which are reputable and others of which are not. If a person claiming to be a cabbie appears to be driving his own car (which doesn't have a meter), either don't get in or establish the fare before you do, be prepared to provide directions to the driver, and cross your fingers.

Ferry

The ferry system is not particularly user-friendly. It is also pricier than other forms of transport. However, for certain trips, such as to the Tower of London, Greenwich, or Kew from Westminster Pier, it is worth the extra hassle and expense for the view from the Thames.

Naturally, guided boat tours of the Thames are also available. Most tours are hop-on hop-off and stop at Westminster, Tower, Greenwich, and Waterloo piers, for a good overview of London. City Cruises (www.citycruises.com) will give a discount with a valid Travel Pass.

National Rail

Regional overland trains connect with Tube stations throughout London. Travel Passes can be used on the trains and count towards the total fare if leaving Zone 2. It is unlikely that a visitor will need to use the trains within London, but day trips will likely require a rail journey. Several of the train stations throughout London individually serve as much traffic as Grand Central station in New York, so ticket ordering can become complicated if you are uncertain from which station within London to depart. It is usually easiest to contact the destination station for journey information.

Get Connected

It's a trip enhancer to be connected. London isn't a place to get away from it all, it's a place to get into it all! You'll want to be able to meet up with new friends, keep tabs on the news, find phone numbers, maps, and opening times, and get on club guest lists.

Mobile Phones

It's easy to walk into the shop of any of the major phone companies (Vodafone, O2, Orange, T-Mobile), pick up a cheap phone, sign up for pay-as-you-go service, and walk out with your own London phone number ready to start making calls. Don't bother setting up international service – a phone card from any corner store is the cheapest way to stay in touch with folks at home (see Phone Cards on the next page). Most importantly, having a mobile is the only way to ensure you'll be able to meet up with new friends again while you're in London. Figure £40 for a basic phone and another £30 for initializing service and starting minutes.

Internet access

There are Internet cafes all over London. The behemoth, Easy Internet (www.easyeverything.com), has 33 locations in London, charges £1 per hour for occasional use, or much less for an extended pass (1, 5, 7, 14, 25, or 30 days, in the neighborhood of £1 per day). Unfortunately, a pass only works at a single location, so be sure to find the one most convenient to your accommodation. Many other net cafes are also fine, but don't get fooled into paying £1 for 10 minutes. Most London sights have very complete websites, which are invaluable for planning a visit. Clubs often have great websites where you can sign up to be on the VIP or guest list.

www.yell.com

This is the online telephone directory for the UK. It's easy to use, includes a good map function, and the search engine works by neighborhood and postcode (e.g. W1), so it's a handy way to find businesses of all kinds throughout London.

Get Connected

Phone Cards

Newsagents in London sell international dialing cards. You shouldn't have to pay more than a couple of pence per minute to call home to the States, so be sure to check the rates and buy a card specializing in North America. Cards can be used with your accommodation phone or your mobile, but not with all pay phones.

Dialing rules

To call a London number printed as +44 (0)20 7123 4567:

Numbers printed	+	44	(0)20	7123 4567
Numbers dialed from US	011	44	20	7123 4567
Numbers dialed from UK			020	7123 4567
Numbers dialed within London				7123 4567
Numbers dialed from Europe	00	44	20	7123 4567

To call a US number printed as (206) 123 4567:

Numbers printed			(206)	123 4567
Numbers dialed from London	00	1	206	123 4567

Note that:
- The "+" is the place holder for the international dialing code.
- The "+" is sometimes omitted or "00" will be printed instead.
- 011 is the international dialing code used from the US.
- 00 is the international dialing code used from Europe, incl. the UK.
- 44 is the UK country code.
- 1 is the US country code *and* the long distance dialing code between cities within the US.
- (0) is the long distance calling code between cities within the UK.
- Parentheses are not always printed around the "0".
- 20 is the London area code.
- 7 is the starting number for central London phone numbers.
- London numbers are sometimes printed 207 123 4567 (tacking the 7 onto the end of the 20), but the same dialing rules apply.
- UK numbers outside of London typically have less than the standard eight digits used within London.

Make Friends

Making friends in London is difficult, not because Londoners are unfriendly, but because they place a high value on wit and being on top of current events, neither of which usually describes the stereotypical American tourist. A little advance planning makes this hurdle much easier to overcome.

Get Savvy
It's surprisingly simple to find out what's hot in London, and fun trip preparation to learn what Londoners are reading, watching, and listening to. Then, when you're down at your new local pub, you'll have something interesting to talk about.

- News: http://news.bbc.co.uk
- Gossip: www.hellomagazine.com
- What's Happening: www.timeout.com/london
- Sports: http://sports.bbc.co.uk
- Bestsellers: www.timesonline.co.uk ➔ Books
- Blockbusters: http://entertainment.timesonline.co.uk ➔ Film
- Chart Toppers: www.hit40.co.uk/chart
- Streaming Pop Radio: www.capitalfm.com
- On the Telly: http://entertainment.timesonline.co.uk ➔TV

Pursue Your Passion
Nothing breaks down social barriers like a common passion (or obsession!). Use Google and www.yell.com to hunt down clubs, classes, groups, societies, events, shops – any meeting place that involves your hobby or interests. You're almost guaranteed to have a good time attending demonstrations, exhibitions, sales, meetings or other events focused on something you already know you enjoy, and hopefully you'll gain the chance to make friends with others who share your love, mission, or vice.

Make Friends

Get Out & Mingle

Now that you're armed with great conversation fuel, go out on-the-town. To keep up with events, art, concerts, film, theatre, sports, the latest bars and restaurants, the club scene, and more you'll want to invest £2.50 at the local newsagent for a copy of *Time Out* each week. There are many imitators, but this weekly periodical is the definitive calendar for what's on in London.

A few tips on smooth interactions when out and about:

- You're likely to have better success if you **dress well**. Even at a relatively casual pub it's highly unlikely that t-shirts and jeans are going to impress. At bars it is unusual to see men in jeans.

- **Insist on buying a round.** While at home it is normal for people to pay individually for their drinks, in the UK (and Ireland) that's highly antisocial and potentially even offensive. When your drink gets low, just ask everyone in the circle what they'd like from the bar. Don't worry, they'll return the favor.

- **Don't bring up American sports**. We're the butt of global jokes for inventing sports that no one else plays. If you're a sports fan, learn about football (soccer), rugby, and cricket before you go.

- **Don't discuss American politics**. America's position as the most powerful country in the world doesn't make us popular, and our foreign policy is often inscrutable to the rest of the world. On top of that, the average perpetually well-informed Brit knows more about American politics than the average sound-byte satiated American, which is a recipe for looking foolish. It can be an alarmingly speedy conversation killer.

- **Sharpen your wit**. Perhaps more than any other country, and certainly more than any other English-speaking country, Brits flirt with words. If you're not particularly clever with turns of phrase, watch some Eddie Izzard DVDs as a pre-trip warm-up.

Make Friends

Avoid Tourists
Make friends with Londoners, not just other tourists.

- Travel in **April/May** or **September/October**, avoiding the horribly humid and crowded summer months when Londoners become justifiably irritated with the number of foreigners crowding their streets and congesting the Tube.
- Don't spend all day sightseeing – **hang out at pubs**, cafes, parks, and in the residential neighborhoods.
- Skip the tourist-only attractions.

Avoid Faux Pas
These tips will also help avoid pickpockets and con artists.

- Do not wear **athletic apparel** (including sneakers, caps, jerseys, t-shirts, warm-ups, fleeces, sports team insignias, etc.) unless going to the gym. Americans generally dress far more casually than Europeans and we are ridiculed for it, *especially* when we wear white sneakers with jeans.
- Do not wear **tourist apparel**, e.g., backpacks, hip packs, sun visors, cameras, etc., and don't go outside with a map or a guidebook prominently in hand.
- Do not **block traffic** on sidewalks or escalators. Stay to the right, be aware of the space that you and your companions are taking up, and don't amble down busy thoroughfares – wait 'til you've arrived at your destination to chat.
- Do not request **customized orders**. Stick to what's shown on the menu and don't forget to tip 10-15%.
- Do not be **arrogantly patriotic**. Never start a sentence with "Back home..." and then complain about Britain. Do not wear anything featuring the Stars & Stripes (God bless them).
- Do not **speak loudly**. Americans are notoriously noisy, particularly on public transportation. Keep your voice down.

Make Friends

Volunteer

Put karma to the test – you won't be let down. Most volunteer organizations in the US will have a counterpart in the UK, so if you're already plugged into a volunteer group at home, look up their sister organization across the pond. Helping out at a church, a charity, or a civic or sporting event is a great way to make friends - you've clearly shown you're a friendly person and you'll have the opportunity to work side-by-side with like-minded folk.

Look Up That Friend-of-a-Friend

Even a very tenuous acquaintance is better than none at all. Do you know anyone that has visited London who may still have contacts there? Does your employer have a branch office with some friendly colleagues? Do you have any long-lost relatives in London? It is more than worth overcoming the natural resistance to contacting a virtual stranger. Any time they may be able share with you will be invaluable, and you can easily assuage any guilt you may feel about imposing by remembering that one day you'll hopefully have the chance to repay their kindness by returning the favor.

Do a London Version of your Home Routine

Pick a day of your trip to live like a Saturday back home. Sleep in. Take your clothes to the launderette. Pick up toothpaste at Boots. Get your film developed at Snappy Snaps. Buy cereal and milk at Sainsbury's or Tesco. Get a haircut at the local salon. Rent a video. Go kick a ball around at the park. Buy an ice cream at the corner store. Read the paper. Take some mail to the post office. Find a pub showing a sports match and have a beer. And all the while, keep an eye open for a friendly face and an opportunity to start a conversation. You seem much more approachable if you're doing something normal, just like a Londoner.

Make Friends

Know Thy History

You'll want to be familiar with the key facts and figures of London's history. You'd be surprised how often this knowledge comes in handy, so here's the cheat sheet from your high school European history class:

- 43 AD: Londinium settled during Roman invasion
- 1042: Edward the Confessor rebuilds Westminster Abbey
- 1066: William of Orange conquers Britain and crowned king
- 1534: Henry VIII declares himself head of the Church
- 1588: Shakespeare begins his dramatic career in London
- 1603: Queen Elizabeth's 45-year reign ends
- 1649: Charles I executed; Oliver Cromwell named Lord Protector
- 1660: Monarchy restored under Charles II
- 1664: Plague kills 20 percent of the population
- 1666: Great Fire destroys 80 percent of London (ending The Plague)
- 1675: Christopher Wren begins work on St. Paul's Cathedral
- 1764: Samuel Johnson compiles the first English Dictionary
- 1805: Admiral Nelson dies in action against Napoleon at Trafalgar
- 1815: Admiral Wellington ends Napoleon's reign at Waterloo
- 1834: Houses of Parliament built
- 1837: Queen Victoria ascends the throne
- 1860: The first installment of Dickens' *Great Expectations* published
- 1888: Jack the Ripper strikes in Whitechapel
- 1901: Doyle's *The Hound of the Baskervilles* published
- 1914 – 1918: WW1
- 1939 – 1945: WW2 – Winston Churchill is Prime Minster
- 1952: Queen Elizabeth II (the current Queen) ascends the throne
- 1979: Margaret Thatcher becomes Britain's first woman Prime Minister
- 1997: Tony Blair is elected Prime Minister

Down the Pub

For most Brits, their "local" is a second home. London has its glitz and glam, but the pub remains the social heart of the city.

Pub Life

Each pub has its own unique character, but there are unifying traits:

- **Regulars** Only the most touristy pubs lack these guests who can usually be found on the same stool with same pint in hand.
- **Sport** match commentary often hums on the telly above the bar, but all conversation stops when the football is on.
- **Fruit Machines** Gambling is a national obsession. Slot (a.k.a. fruit) machines and golf arcade game Golden Tee are ubiquitous.
- **Diversions** Even sharks have trouble with billiards – the pockets are so small. Darts and table football are more familiar pastimes.
- **Music** Many pubs have a jukebox, and a few will host live music on weekends. Most pubs are not licensed for dancing, however.
- **Quizzes** Brits are renowned for their love of minutia and trivia. Many pubs host a very lively quiz night once a week.

Etiquette

Naturally, such a central part of the culture has its own protocols.

- **Rounds** When socializing avoid committing a serious offense – be sure to take your turn buying drinks for the group.
- **Ordering** It's rare to have table service. Ordering drinks and food takes place at the bar. Keeping a tab for the evening is common.
- **Tipping** Although tipping is rare, it's polite to offer to buy the bartender a drink and leave the cash to cover it.
- **Playing** If someone is on the billiards table, it's customary to offer to play the winner and set change on the table.
- **Pulling** Flirting is referred to as "chatting up" or "pulling" and it's all about sparring with wit. Visitors should be concerned about appearing aggressive rather than the opposite.

Down the Pub

- **Smoking** Londoners are slowly breaking the habit, and it is likely that in the relatively near future smoking will be prohibited in pubs.
- **Hours** For decades, pubs have been open from 11-11, and closing time is strict. Laws are changing to allow later operating hours.
- **Don'ts** Don't be shy about starting a conversation, but don't fail to bow out if it's not being happily reciprocated. Don't touch people, and don't pick fights. Don't get obnoxiously drunk.

Libations
It's rare to hear the word "beer". Pints come in several varieties.

- **Ale** Like non-carbonated beer, locals find it delicious
- **Lager** What most Americans refer to as beer
- **Stout** The most famous version of this dark beer is Guinness
- **Shandy** Lagers can be diluted to half strength for lightweights
- **Gin** The English love their gin and tonic (known as G&T)
- **Spirits** Bars and pubs are separate animals in London, and a few pubs do not even offer hard alcohol, so stick to basics
- **Mixers** Tonic is common, Sprite/7Up are called lemonade
- **Wine** Pubs typically carry one or two whites and reds
- **Alcopops** These bottled mixed drinks are for ladies only
- **Cocktails** Unheard of at the pub

Fare
England's most amusing vocabulary comes from the pub kitchen.

- **Bangers 'n' Mash** = sausages, mashed potatoes, and gravy
- **Toad in the Hole** = sausages baked in a Yorkshire pudding
- **Yorkshire Pudding** = airy pastry, usually a side to meat

Down the Pub

- **Jacket Potato** = baked potato with a wide range of toppings
- **Fish 'n' Chips** = always served with peas
- **Sunday Roast** = best bargain in London, a big roast meal of beef, pork, or lamb, with potatoes, vegetables, and Yorkshire pudding
- **Pastas** = a disappointing choice at the pub
- **Curries** = Chicken Tikka Masala is taking over as the national dish
- **Sandwiches** = usually the "salad" variety (mixed with mayonnaise)
- **Pudding** = dessert, such as Spotted Dick and Roly Poly
- **Snacks** = crisps (potato chips) and nuts, look for unusual flavors like roast beef, tomato, shrimp, and pickle

More recently the gastropub has arrived on the scene, typically tonier than the standard pub, with a restaurant kitchen, varied menu, and higher prices.

Pub Chains
Most pubs are no longer independent, and a few of the chains have developed a distinct identity throughout London.

- **Pitcher & Piano, Slug & Lettuce** –toney and modern
- **O'Neills, Walkabout** – geared towards frat party behavior
- **Feathers** – somewhere between the previous two
- **Scream** – aimed at students, with bright colors and cheap menu
- **Witherspoons** – low prices, family specials, a bit like Denny's

Speak Well

Proper Pronunciation

Londoners love to poke fun at American accents, and our pronunciation of place names in particular.

- **-bury** = bree (Canonbury = CAN-on-bree, Bloomsbury = BLOOMS-bree)
- **-cester** = ster (Leicester = LESS-ter, Gloucester = GLOSS-ter)
- **-ham** = um (Clapham = CLAP-um, Fulham = FULL-um, Buckingham = BUCK-ing-um, Tottenham = TOT-num)
- **-shire** = shur (Cheshire = CHESH-ur, Lincolnshire = LINK-un-shur)
- **-wark, -wick, -witch** = uk, ick, itch (Southwark = SUTH-uk, Warwick = WAR-ick, Greenwich = GREN-itch, *but* Gatwick = GAT-wick)
- **Borough** = BURR-ah
- **Brixton** = BRICKS-tun
- **Clerkenwell** = CLARK-n-well
- **Cornwall** = CORN-wul
- **Edinburgh** = ED-in-bra
- **Fitzrovia** = fits-ROVE-ya
- **Hampstead** = HAMPS-tud
- **Islington** = IZZ-ling-tun
- **Lambeth** = LAM-buth
- **Marylebone** = MAHRL-uh-bone
- **Norfolk** = NORF-uk
- **Shoreditch** = SHORED-itch
- **Spitalfields** = Spittle Fields
- **Thames** = TEMS
- **Z** = ZED

Warning: Don't under any circumstances go overboard and think it's okay to fake a British accent while in London – it is not!

Speak Well

English Vocabulary

While the language barrier across the pond is *wee*, the variations can be amusing. A *cheeky* resource on the topic is *The American-British British-American Dictionary*, but these are the essentials:

People
- **Bird** = gal
- **Bloke** = guy
- **Mate** = friend

Adjectives
- **Bladdered, Legless, Smashed** = drunk
- **Knackered** = exhausted
- **Gutted** = sorely disappointed
- **Brilliant** = fabulous
- **Smart** = sleek, professional
- **Fit** = attractive, hot
- **Keen** = very interested, ambitious
- **Keen on** = very interested in somebody (crush)
- **Ginger, Ginge** = redhead
- **Posh** = rich, snobbish, expensive

Places
- **Loo, WC, Toilet** = restroom
- **High Street** = Main Street
- **Off License, Newsagent** = corner store + liquor store

Things
- **Queue** = line
- **Quid** = £pound
- **Elevenses** = hunger at 11 o'clock (or the snack to cure it)
- **Biscuit** = cookie
- **Crack** = good fun
- **Holiday** = vacation

Speak Well

Interjections
- **You alright?** = hello, how's it going, what's up
- **Cheers** = thank-you
- **Innit** = that's right, isn't that right
- **Can't be arsed, can't be bothered** = no interest in doing x
- **Go tits up, go pear-shaped** = go awry
- **Taking the piss / having a laugh** = pulling one's leg

Verbs
- **Blag** = steal
- **Ring** = call
- **Post** = mail
- **Fancy** = desire
- **Pull, Chat Up** = flirt
- **Snog** = kiss

Insults & Naughty Words
- **Twee, Naff** = dorky
- **Dodgy** = shady
- **Manky** = disgusting
- **Tart, Minx, Slag** = slut
- **Tarted Up** = dressed sexy
- **Wanker** = jerk
- **Prat** = snob
- **Bloody** = effing
- **Pants** = bull sh*t
- **Fanny** = a lady's you-know-what

Clothes
- **Pants, Knickers** = panties
- **Trousers** = pants
- **Trainers** = sneakers

Save Money

A few simple considerations can save a significant amount of money – two people could **save £1,250+ per week with little to no extra effort!** That's a lot of shopping!

Save £50+ per person per week – Lodging

Accommodation is the most painful expense of visiting London, especially when so little time will be spent at the lodgings, there's so much to see and do. However, it's important not to skimp – staying in an inconvenient or dysfunctional location will have a serious negative impact on the trip.

- **B&Bs** – a clean, comfortable, convenient B&B en suite double room needn't cost more than £75 per night. A comparable room at a hotel could easily cost £125 or more. For ideas and help see the Accommodation section or check www.bulldogclub.com and www.lhslondon.co.uk.

- **House swap** – particularly for travelers with some flexibility and planning on an extended stay, a house swap provides huge savings. Be very careful about choosing location – if the postcode does not start with N1, NW1, W1, W2, WC, EC, or SW1 it may be prohibitively far away from the center or in a bad neighborhood. Start at http://london.craigslist.org.

- **Off-season** – Most accommodation is around 10 percent cheaper during January through April and October/November.

Save £50+ per person per week – Meals

Food is a huge expense in London. These tricks can reduce the bill:

- **Breakfast** – Staying at a **B&B** is the easiest way to reduce both lodging and food costs, as the typical breakfast includes cold cereal, fruit, eggs, bacon, sausages, mushrooms, tomatoes, toast, tea, and coffee. Alternatively, seek out a crowded neighborhood **café** – often that same breakfast will cost only £2.50.

Save Money

- **Lunch** – **Caffe Nero**, **EAT**, **Giraffe**, and **Pret a Manger** specialize in sandwiches and other lunch fare. Grocery store **Marks & Spencer** and pharmacy **Boots** frequently have a lunch section where you can pick up an inexpensive sandwich, snack and drink. Museums, many churches, and some public buildings have simple cafes, which are typically a very good value. DIY lunch from supermarkets Sainsbury's, Tesco, Waitrose, and Marks & Spencer are all reliably cheap.

- **Dinner** – Most pubs have at least a simple menu featuring bangers 'n mash (sausages and mashed potatoes), fish 'n chips, burgers, and other fare. So-called gastropubs retain the pub atmosphere but focus on their food and have a more extensive menu, sometimes still fairly cheap (but sometimes not). The pub is definitely the place to go early on Sunday afternoon for a huge, tasty and reasonable roast dinner. Many restaurants will do a *prix fixe* menu during early dinner hours, so keep an eye open for the signboard advertisements.

Transportation – save £100+ per person per week

Taking cabs requires the least effort but is easily the most expensive form of transport (besides renting a car, which in London is abject foolishness). Reduce in-city travel costs by buying in bulk and taking a few minutes to get to know the Tube.

- **Travel Cards** – A 3-Day Zones 1 and 2 Travel Card can be purchased at any Tube station for only £15 for use on the Tube, buses, and rail any where in Zones 1 and 2, and also counts towards the cost of transport outside of Zone 2.

- **Night Buses** – London's buses run all night, so if you're staying out late a quick check on the bus routes can save you cab fare.

- **Off-season** – Plane tickets during January through April and October/November are usually cheaper.

Save Money

Save £50+ per person per week – Entertainment

Some shows are worth the full ticket price – how often do you get the chance to see Alan Rickman or Judi Dench on stage? But otherwise:

- **Half-Price Day-Of Tickets** – if there are tickets left on the day of a performance, it's likely they'll be made available for half-price or less. The tkts booth in Leicester Square sells half-price tickets for Theatreland productions starting at 10 am. Tickets to long running musicals (Phantom, Les Mis, Chicago, etc.) are almost always available; critically acclaimed new shows often sell out, but sometimes opportunists get lucky with cheap seats. The Royal Opera House sells any available tickets from their box office starting at 4 pm.

    Note that Shakespeare's Globe Theatre and other venues do not reduce the price of tickets on the day of the performance.

- **Pub Theater** – There are dozens of pub theaters throughout London. Production can be below the quality of the big name theaters but the level of acting often matches or surpasses what can be found in Theatreland. Compare £5 tix to £50 and it's worth the gamble. And the beer's cheaper!

Save £50+ per person per week – Sights

Many London sights are £5-10 or more to visit, but these are free!

- **Museums** – National museums (British Museum, Museum of London, National Gallery, National Portrait Gallery, Tate Britain, Tate Modern, V&A, and Wallace Collection) are free.

- **Churches** – Major churches charge admission for entrance and additional fees for tours. Attend a gratis service or lunchtime concert instead.

- **Courts** – The public may watch trials held in the Central Criminal Court (Old Bailey) free of charge.

- **Parliament** – Attending the debates in both Houses is free.

Save Money

Shopping – save 50%+
Threads aren't cheap in London, but there are a handful of ways to find potential bargains:

- **Petticoat Lane** – This street market, just south of Old Spitalfields Market, primarily sells trash. However, it is also occasionally a liquidation spot for high street shops where lucky folks have snagged £50 skirts, tops and trousers for £5. If in the neighborhood it's worth doing a fly-by.

- **Second-Hand** – A number of renowned second-hand shops in London include Bertie Golightly, Catwalk, and Rokit. Brick Lane, Camden Market, Hampstead High Street, and Portobello Road all have numerous vintage and used clothes shops.

- **Clearance Outlets** – The most famous clearance shop is Browns Labels for Less in Mayfair, which is the outlet for unsold designer clothes from their flagship store around the corner.

- **Sales** – High street shops generally have big sales in January and July, so if in London during those times don't miss the bargains.

- **Sample Sales** – After London Fashion Week the designers sell samples, typically at the Earls Court Exhibition Center. It's a bit chaotic but definitely desirable for die-hard fashionistas.

Basics – save 10% - 50%
It's rarely a good idea to purchase anything from souvenir shops or train stations. When looking for staples such as water, snacks, pain relievers, toiletries, magazines, and the like, keep an eye open for grocery stores such as Sainsburys or Tesco or chemist (pharmacist) Boots.

Discover Secret London

Many visitors to London walk past the following secret treasures without even noticing them. A savvy observer will keep eyes open for:

Blue Plaques

Blue pizza-sized tiles adorn over 760 buildings in London, celebrating illustrious residents of the past (from the likes of Lennon to Gandhi) and their homes. A complete list of names and locations is available at www.englishheritage.org.uk → Blue Plaques.

Cabmen's Shelters

These small green huts stand in the center of busy streets, surrounded by black cabs. Starting in 1875 they were erected to provide shelter and food for cabmen during their break times, and they continue as second homes to the famed London cabbies. Only a handful exist today – prominent ones are across the street from the V&A and at Warwick Avenue in Little Venice. Access is exclusive to cab drivers, but lucky passers by may catch a glimpse of the cozy yet simple interior through an open door.

Canal Boats

Canals provided critical freight transport throughout the UK before the Industrial Revolution and the arrival of the steam engine. Today, those seeking a simpler London lifestyle live on the canals in narrow boats, and many more vacation on them. Picturesque access points to the Regents Canal are at Angel, Little Venice, and Regents Park. More information about the canals is at the British Waterways website, www.britishwaterways.co.uk.

Door Awnings

Before streetlamps became widely used, London addresses were recognized at night by a unique shadow cast through a fan-shaped window above the front door. In well-preserved neighborhoods (such as Hampstead) the differently patterned windows can still be seen crowning the doorways along the rows of stately homes.

Discover Secret London

Royal Warrants
Since 1155 tradesmen who provide goods directly to the Royal Family have been awarded a Royal Warrant, which is renewable every five years. Currently around 800 Royal Warrant holders display the phrase "By appointment to" (with the name of the Royal and corresponding coat of arms) on their product packaging, stationery and in their shop windows. More information is available at www.royalwarrants.org.uk.

Defunct Tube Stations
There are many Underground stations no longer in use, though the distinctive red tile facades are still visible on their respective streets, such as Aldwych, Down Street, and Brompton Road. More information is available at www.subbrit.org.uk. London's Transport Museum occasionally provides tours, so interested parties should contact them in advance. www.ltmuseum.co.uk

Cast and Wrought Iron Trimming
Take a close look at the copious cast- and wrought-iron found on buildings throughout London. There are horse hitches, gas lamps, shoe scrapers, pineapples (a sign of hospitality), gates, and more. You'll be sure to spot something whose use defies guessing. Be sure to enjoy the gates to Shakespeare's Globe, a masterful set that includes an icon from each of the Bard's many plays.

Unusual Museums
London has literally hundreds of museums and galleries. Many are the former homes of famed London residents (Keats, Faraday, Freud, Dickens, Johnson). Others are dedicated to obscure or unusual subjects (fans, clocks, transport, medicine, tea). Some of these museums are mentioned in this guidebook, but many are not. Keep a sharp eye for brown and white street signs with a walking man or acorns depicted – these indicate that a museum or historical site is close at hand. You never know what you're going to find!

Emergency Information / Personal Safety

Dial 999 or 112
This is the equivalent of 911 in the US. Call for emergencies requiring the services of police, ambulance, firefighters, coast guard, or rescue.

Look Right Before Crossing
Remember that traffic comes from the opposite direction in London, and pedestrians do not automatically have the right of way. Most street corners will have either "Look Left" or "Look Right" painted in the road as appropriate, but if not – remember to **look right**!

Commute Wisely
Levels of violent crime in London remain low, but it is prudent to avoid being alone at night with valuables. A few tips:
- Know your night transport plan for the evening ahead of time
- Do not dress like a tourist (especially no backpacks or hip packs)
- Avoid poorly lit areas
- Avoid empty train and Tube carriages
- Carry a mobile phone
- Sit near the driver or conductor

American Embassy
Contact the Embassy for assistance with lost passports. Be sure to bring a photocopy of your passport on the trip.

American Embassy, 24 Grosvenor Square, W1A 1AE / +44 (0)20 7499 9000 www.usembassy.org.uk / M-F, by appt.

Health & Medical Attention
American visitors are not entitled to free health services under the NHS and must bring a photocopy of their travel insurance policy. In case of emergency, dial 999 or 112. Free medical advice and information on contacting doctors is available from NHS Direct, at +44 (0)870 4647 or www.nhsdirect.nhs.uk.

Index

2 Willow Road	HC	
25 Canonbury Lane	I	
333	SS	

A
The Abingdon	KS
A&D Gallery	MF
Accessorize	MS, I
Alexander McQueen	MS
Almeida Theatre	I
Aquarium	SS
Arsenal F.C.	I
Ashburnham Arms	G

B
Baltic	SL
Bamboula	BrC
Bank of England Museum	C
Bar Meze	BrC
Barry House Hotel	92
Bars (see Nightlife)	
Bartok	HC
Battersea Park	CF
BBC Shop	MS
Bertie Golightly	KS
Beyond Retro	SS
Bibendum	CF
Big Ben	W
Biggles Sausages	MF
Blagden Fishmongers	MF
Blakemore Hotel	93
Blue Elephant	CF
Bluu	SS
Bootsy Brogan's	CF
Borough Market	SL
Bramah Tea & Coffee Museum	SL
British Library	BlC
British Museum	BlC
Brixton Academy	BrC
Brixton Market	BrC
Brockwell Park	BrC
Browns Labels for Less	MS
Burberry	KS
Butler & Wilson	CF
The Button Queen	MF
Byron Hotel	93

C
Cabinet War Rooms & Churchill Museum	W
Caernarvon Castle	HC
Café Naz	SS
Cafes (see Restaurants)	
Caffe Nero	C, MS, HC
Camden Markets	HC
Camden Passage Antiques Market	I
Canonbury	I
Cantaloupe	SS
Cantina Italia	I
Cargo	SS
Catwalk	MF
Central Criminal Court	HE
Chelsea F.C.	CF
Chelsea Physic Garden	CF
Cigala	BlC
Cittie of Yorke	BlC
Clapham Common	BrC
Clockwork	I
Clubs (see nightlife)	
Coffee Republic	MS
Comfort Station	SS
Cotton's Restaurant	HC
Courtezan	CF
Courtauld Gallery	HE
The Cow	HN
Craven Gardens Hotel	92
Cru	SS
Crypt Café	W
Cutty Sark	G

D
Daunt's Books	MF
Debonair Debonair	HN
Delmere	93
Diverse	I
The Drawing Room	BrC
Dusk	MF

E
The Eagle	BlC
EAT	C, HE, MS, W
Elbow Room	I
Electric Ballroom	HC
Electric Brasserie	HN
Elgin	HN
Embassy	I

Bloomsbury/**C**lerkenwell	BlC	58	**H**olland Park/**N**otting Hill	HN	48
Brixton/**C**lapham	BrC	66	**I**slington	I	74
Chelsea/**F**ulham	CF	40	**K**nightsbridge/**S**outh Ken	KS	44
City	C	30	**M**arylebone/**F**itzrovia	MF	52
Covent Garden/**S**trand	CS	23	**M**ayfair/**S**oho	MS	18
Greenwich	G	79	**S**horeditch/**S**pitalfields	SS	62
Hampstead/**C**amden	HC	70	**S**outhwark/**L**ambeth	SL	34
Holborn/**E**mbankment	HE	26	**W**estminster	W	14

Entertainment / Sports
- Almeida Theatre — I
- Arsenal F.C. — I
- Brixton Academy — BrC
- Chelsea F.C. — CF
- Globe Theatre — SL
- Hen & Chicks — I
- The King's Head — I
- Little Angel — I
- Lord's Cricket Ground — MF
- Official London Theatre / tkts — CS
- Old Red Lion — I
- Royal Albert Hall — KS
- Royal Festival Hall — SL
- Royal National Theatre — SL
- Royal Opera House — CS
- Sadler's Wells — I
- Screen on the Green — I
- Shakespeare's Globe Theatre — SL
- Wigmore Hall — MF
- Estorick Collection — I
- Euphorium — I

F
- Fabric — BlC
- Fan Museum — G
- Faux Pas — 104
- Fenton House — HC
- Fiesta Havana — CF, MS
- Florence Nightingale Museum — SL
- Fluid — BlC
- Fortnum & Mason — MS
- Foundling Museum — BlC
- Fox & Hounds — CF
- French Connection (FCUK) — I, MS
- The Fridge — BrC
- Frockbrokers — SS

G
- Galleries (see museums)
- the garden — I
- George Inn — SL
- Gilbert Collection — HE
- Giovanni's — CS
- Gipsy Moth — G
- Giraffe — I, HC, MF
- Globe Theatre — SL
- The Grand — BrC
- The Grapes — G
- Greenwich Market — G
- Gresham Hyde Park — 93
- Guildhall — C

H
- Hampstead Heath — HC
- Harvey Nichols — KS
- Heaven — CS
- Heights at the St. Georges Hotel — MS
- Hen & Chicks — I
- Highgate Cemetery — 83
- Holland Park — HN
- Hyde Park — KS

I
- Inside — G
- Imperial War Museum — SL
- Isolabella — BlC
- The Ivy — MS

J
- Jimmy Choo — MS

K
- Katharine Bird — BrC
- Kensington Gardens — KS
- Kensington Palace — KS
- Kenwood House — HC
- Kew Gardens — 83
- The King's Head — I
- Kingsway Park Hotel — 93
- Koko — HC
- Konaki — BlC

L
- La Pampa — BrC
- Labour & Wait — SS
- The Lamb — BlC
- Lambeth Palace — SL
- Landsdowne — HC
- Lavender — BrC
- Leadenhall Market — C
- Leighton House Museum — HN
- Liberty — MS
- Lincoln's Inn — HE
- Little Angel — I
- London Eye — SL
- London Silver Vaults — HE
- Lonsdale — HN
- Loop Bar — MS
- Lord's Cricket Ground — MF
- Lulu Guinness — KS

M
- Mango Room — HC
- Manolo Blahnik — KS
- Markets (see Shops)
- Market Porter — SL
- Marquise of Granby — MF
- Freemason's Arms — HC
- Mass — BrC
- Matches — HN
- Ministry of Sound — SL
- Mise en Place — BrC
- Mobile Telephones — 100
- Montmartre — I
- Monument — C
- Mornington Hotel — 93
- Museum of Garden History — SL
- Museum of London — C
- **Museums / Galleries**
  - A&D Gallery — MF
  - Bank of England Museum — C
  - Bramah Tea & Coffee Museum — SL
  - British Library — BlC
  - British Museum — BlC
  - Cabinet War Rooms & Churchill Museum — W
  - Courtauld Gallery — HE
  - Estorick Collection — I
  - Fan Museum — G
  - Fenton House — HC

Florence Nightingale Museum	SL
Foundling Museum	BIC
Gilbert Collection	HE
Imperial War Museum	SL
Museum of Garden History	SL
Museum of London	C
National Gallery	W
National Maritime Museum	G
National Portrait Gallery	W
Old Royal Naval College	G
Old Royal Observatory	G
Rangers House	G
Saatchi Gallery	SL
Sir John Soane Museum	HE
Somerset House	HE
Tate Britain	W
Tate Modern	SL
V&A (Victoria & Albert Museum)	KS
Wallace Collection	MF
White Cube	SS
Whitechapel Art Gallery	SS

N

National Gallery	W
National Maritime Museum	G
National Portrait Gallery	W
Next	MS

Nightlife

25 Canonbury Lane	I
333	SS
Aquarium	SS
Baltic	SL
Bartok	HC
Bluu	SS
Caernarvon Castle	HC
Cantaloupe	SS
Cargo	SS
Clockwork	I
Dusk	HN
Elbow Room	I
Electric Ballroom	HC
Embassy	I
Fabric	BIC
Fiesta Havana	CF, MS
Fluid	BIC
The Fridge	BrC
The Grand	BrC
Heaven	CS
Koko	HC
Loop Bar	MS
Lonsdale	HN
Mass	BrC
Ministry of Sound	SL
Nordic	MF
Notting Hill Arts Club	HN
On Anon	MS
Paragon	MS
South Side	MF
Tiger Tiger	MS
Turnmills	BIC
Underworld	HC
W'Sens	MS
Nordic	MF
Norfolk Plaza Hotel	93
Notting Hill Arts Club	HN

O

Oasis	I, MS
Official London Theatre / tkts	CS
Old Bailey	HE
Old Red Lion	I
Old Royal Naval College	G
Old Royal Observatory	G
Old Spitalfields Market	SS
On Anon	MS
The Orangery	KS
Orrery	MF
Oxo Tower	SL

P

Palace of Westminster	W
Paragon	MS
Park Lodge Hotel	93

Parks

Battersea Park	CF
Brockwell Park	BrC
Chelsea Physic Garden	CF
Clapham Common	BrC
Hampstead Heath	HC
Holland Park	HN
Hyde Park	KS
Kensington Gardens	KS
Kew Gardens	83
Parliament Hill	HC
Postman's Gardens	C
Primrose Hill	MF
Regents Park	MF
Richmond Park	83
St. James's Park	W

Bloomsbury/Clerkenwell	BIC	58	Holland Park/Notting Hill	HN	48
Brixton/Clapham	BrC	66	Islington	I	74
Chelsea/Fulham	CF	40	Knightsbridge/South Ken	KS	44
City	C	30	Marylebone/Fitzrovia	MF	52
Covent Garden/Strand	CS	23	Mayfair/Soho	MS	18
Greenwich	G	79	Shoreditch/Spitalfields	SS	62
Hampstead/Camden	HC	70	Southwark/Lambeth	SL	34
Holborn/Embankment	HE	26	Westminster	W	14

Parliament	W	Coffee Republic	MS	Seconda Mano	I
Parliament Hill	HC	Cotton's Restaurant	HC	Shakespeare's Globe	
Patio	KS	The Cow	HN	Theatre	SL

Parliament — W
Parliament Hill — HC
Patio — KS
Perseverance — BlC
Phillip Somerville — MF
Pierre Victoire — MS
Pizza Express — CS, MS
Portobello Green Arcade — HN
Portobello Market — HN
Postman's Gardens — C
Pret a Manger — C, HE, W
Primrose Hill — MF
Providores — MF

Pubs
 Ashburnham Arms — G
 Bootsy Brogan's — CF
 Canonbury — I
 Cittie of Yorke — BlC
 The Eagle — BlC
 Elgin — HN
 Fox & Hounds — CF
 Freemason's Arms — HC
 the garden — I
 George Inn — SL
 Gipsy Moth — G
 The Grapes — G
 The Lamb — BlC
 Market Porter — SL
 Marquise of Granby — MF
 Perseverance — BlC
 Royal Oak — SL
 Townhouse — KS
 Waxy O'Conners — MS

R
Rangers House — G
Regents Park — MF
Restaurants / Cafes
 The Abingdon — KS
 Bamboula — BrC
 Bar Meze — BrC
 Bibendum — CF
 Blue Elephant — CF
 Café Naz — SS
 Caffe Nero — C, MS, HC
 Cantina Italia — I
 Cigala — BlC

Coffee Republic — MS
Cotton's Restaurant — HC
The Cow — HN
Cru — SS
Crypt Café — W
The Drawing Room — BrC
EAT — C, HE, MS, W
Electric Brasserie — HN
Euphorium — I
Fortnum & Mason — MS
Giovanni's — CS
Giraffe — I, HC, MF
Heights at the St.
 Georges Hotel — MS
Inside — G
The Ivy — MS
Isolabella — BlC
Konaki — BlC
La Pampa — BrC
Landsdowne — HC
Lavender — BrC
Mango Room — HC
Mise en Place — BrC
Montmartre — I
The Orangery — KS
Orrery — MF
Oxo Tower — SL
Patio — KS
Pierre Victoire — MS
Pizza Express — CS, MS
Pret a Manger — C, HE, W
Providores — MF
Sea Cow — BrC
The Troubadour — CF
Wells — HC
Richmond Park — 83
Rokit — SS
Royal Albert Hall — KS
Royal Festival Hall — SL
Royal National Theatre — SL
Royal Oak — SL
Royal Opera House — CS

S
Saatchi Gallery — SL
Sadler's Wells — I
Screen on the Green — I
Sea Cow — BrC

Seconda Mano — I
Shakespeare's Globe
 Theatre — SL
Shops / Markets
 Accessorize — MS, I
 Alexander McQueen — MS
 BBC Shop — MS
 Bertie Golightly — KS
 Beyond Retro — SS
 Biggles Sausages — MF
 Blagden
  Fishmongers — MF
 Borough Market — SL
 Brixton Market — BrC
 Browns Labels for Less — MS
 Burberry — KS
 Butler & Wilson — CF
 The Button Queen — MF
 Camden Markets — HC
 Camden Passage
  Antiques Market — I
 Catwalk — MF
 Comfort Station — SS
 Courtezan — CF
 Daunt's Books — MF
 Debonair Debonair — HN
 Diverse — I
 French Connection
  (FCUK) — I, MS
 Frockbrokers — SS
 Greenwich Market — G
 Harvey Nichols — KS
 Jimmy Choo — MS
 Katharine Bird — BrC
 Labour & Wait — SS
 Leadenhall Market — C
 Liberty — MS
 London Silver Vaults — HE
 Lulu Guinness — KS
 Manolo Blahnik — KS
 Matches — HN
 Next — MS
 Oasis — I, MS
 Old Spitalfields Market — SS
 Phillip Somerville — MF

Portobello Green Arcade	HN	St. Paul's Cathedral	HE	The Lamb	BIC
Portobello Market	HN	Swiss Re (The Gherkin)	C	The Orangery	KS
Rokit	SS	Thames Flood Barrier	G	The Troubadour	CF
Seconda Mano	I	Tower of London	C	Theatre (see Entertainment)	
Tallulah	I	Westminster Abbey	W		
Top Shop	MS	Sir John Soane Museum	HE	Tiger Tiger	MS
V V Rouleaux	MF			Top Shop	MS
Vivienne Westwood	MS	Somerset House	HE	Tower of London	C
		South Side	MF	Townhouse	KS
Wink	SS	Sports (see Entertainment)		Transportation	98

Sights

2 Willow Road	HC	St. Brides	HE	Turnmills	BIC
Big Ben	W	St. James's Park	W		
Central Criminal Court	HE	St. Martin-in-the-Fields	W	**U**	
		St. Mary-le-Bow	C	Underworld	HC
Cutty Sark	G	St. Mary-le-Strand	HE		
Guildhall	C	St. Paul's Cathedral	HE	**V**	
Highgate Cemetery	83	Swiss Re (The Gherkin)	C	V V Rouleaux	MF
Kensington Palace	KS			V&A (Victoria & Albert Museum)	KS
Kenwood House	HC	**T**			
Lambeth Palace	SL	Tallulah	I	Vivienne Westwood	MS
Leighton House Museum	HN	Tate Britain	W		
		Tate Modern	SL	**W**	
Lincoln's Inn	HE	Telephones	100	W'Sens	MS
London Eye	SL	Thames Flood Barrier	G	Wallace Collection	MF
Monument	C	The Abingdon	KS	Waxy O'Conners	MS
Old Bailey	HE	The Button Queen	MF	Wells	HC
Palace of Westminster	W	The Cow	HN	Westminster Abbey	W
		The Drawing Room	BrC	White Cube	SS
Parliament	W	The Eagle	BIC	Whitechapel Art Gallery	SS
St. Brides	HE	The Fridge	BrC	Wigmore Hall	MF
St. Martin-in-the-Fields	W	the garden	I	Wink	SS
		The Grand	BrC		
St. Mary-le-Bow	C	The Grapes	G	**XYZ**	
St. Mary-le-Strand	HE	The Ivy	MS	Ye Olde Cheshire Cheese	HE
		The King's Head	I		

Bloomsbury/Clerkenwell	BIC	58	**Holland Park/Notting Hill**	HN	48
Brixton/Clapham	BrC	66	**Islington**	I	74
Chelsea/Fulham	CF	40	**Knightsbridge/South Ken**	KS	44
City	C	30	**Marylebone/Fitzrovia**	MF	52
Covent Garden/Strand	CS	23	**Mayfair/Soho**	MS	18
Greenwich	G	79	**Shoreditch/Spitalfields**	SS	62
Hampstead/Camden	HC	70	**Southwark/Lambeth**	SL	34
Holborn/Embankment	HE	26	**Westminster**	W	14

Notes and Recommendations from Friends:

Notes and Recommendations from Friends:

Notes and Recommendations from Friends:

_____

_____

_____

_____

_____

_____

_____

_____

_____

_____

_____

_____

Thanks are in order to a great many people. To Paul, Beverly, and Rebecca Carlson for their encouragement, ideas and support; to Roberta Cruger, Robyn Winters, Jennifer Aldrich, and Brad Weikel for their hard work; to Paul Gilbert for making it possible for me to live and work abroad; to all my London friends who helped me to be an insider, especially Nicola Mills; and to everyone who came to visit, giving me the idea in the first place.

-Bethany Carlson

Quick Order Form

Online: www.metropolismoxie.com
By mail: PO Box 19477, Seattle WA 98109

Title	Qty.	Cost	Total
London Moxie		$13.99	$.
Shipping & Handling *($4 first item, $2 per item after)*			$.
Sales Tax			$.
TOTAL			$.

Please include check or charge payment with this form.
❑ VISA   ❑ Master Card

Name _____

Card Number _____

Expiration Date _____

Ship to the following address:

Name _____

Address _____

City _____ State _____ Zip _____